CW00494665

About the Author

Herbert Herzmann was born in Vienna, Austria. He studied German literature and history at the Universities of Salzburg and Vienna. From 1975 to 2006 he was a senior lecturer in German at University College Dublin.

His publications include numerous articles and books on German and Austrian literature and theatre.

In 2006 tredition published his book on the question of national identity: *Nationale Identität. Mythos und Wirklichkeit am Beispiel Österreichs.*

He lives in Dublin and Vienna. His hobbies are travel, mountain walking and climbing.

Why this book?

One need not fly to the end of the world and risk life and limb to experience adventures. A week's cycling tour, a drive of several days by car without a clear plan, a hut to hut walk in the Alps or the exploration of a foreign country under one's own steam can be very exciting. The independent traveller may at times face difficulties, as things do not always turn out as expected. However, the reward will consist of surprises and intense experiences. Maybe this book will encourage some readers who are reluctant to travel independently to go out and take on the world.

Parallel to this edition, a German-language version is published by tredition under the title *Reiseabenteuer 1950-2018. Europa, die Americas und Africa.*

The most dangerous of all worldviews is the worldview of people who have not looked at the world. Alexander von Humboldt

Herbert Herzmann

Travel Adventures
1950 - 2018

Europe, the Americas and Africa

www.tredition.de

© 2021 Herbert Herzmann

Verlag: tredition GmbH, Hamburg

ISBN:
978-3-347-22900-6 (Paperback)
978-3-347-22901-3 (Hardcover)
978-3-347-22902-0 (E-Book)

Bibliografische Information der Deutschen Nationalbibliothek:

Die Deutsche Nationalbibliothek verzeichnet diese Publikation in der Deutschen Nationalbibliografie; detaillierte bibliografische Daten sind im Internet über http://dnb.

Information der Deutschen Nationalbibliothek:
Die Deutsche Nationalbibliothek verzeichnet diese Publikation in der Deutschen Nationalbibliografie; detaillierte bibliografische Daten sind im Internet über http://dnb.d-nb.de abrufbar.

Contents

Pictures

Thanks

Travelling in good company increases the joy and diminishes the pain and frustration if things go wrong. I am very grateful to all who have accompanied me on my journeys over the years and to those who have been my hosts in faraway places. Many of them figure in this book. Here I would like to mention three of them: my father Albert Herzmann, my uncle Erich Braumüller, and my wife Ursula Willig. My father planted the seed of *wanderlust* in me when he was reminiscing about his holidays by the Adriatic Sea in Croatia before the Second World War. Uncle Erich has made me love the mountains. Ursula has been a superb travel companion over the past four decades.

My first readers were Ursula, Gray Cahill and Siobhan Parkenson. Their comments and critique have helped me a lot. David Herman, David Jabobs and Gray Cahill undertook the arduous task of proofreading and helping me with my English. I would like to say a big thank you to all of them!

Prologue

Dear Reader,

Apparently you like to travel. If not, then you would not be reading this book. But what do you expect from a trip? Are you seeking the security of the familiar enriched by sunshine and a deep blue sea, or are you looking for adventures? If you belong to the latter category and not take adventure to mean playing with death this is probably the right book for you. Opening up to new experiences may not be entirely risk-free but it enriches life and creates precious memories. If, on the other hand, you prefer lying on a sunny beach and have no desire to explore the country where you are holidaying, I hope that reading this will encourage you to be a little more daring. Maybe you are worried that you will not be able to communicate in a foreign language or that you may be robbed or get into other difficulties. Travelling under your own steam is not as dangerous as you may think. You do not have to risk life and limb by riding on your bicycle through Africa or snowboarding from a Himalayan peak in order to have an adventure.

I always loved travelling. By this I do not only mean visiting faraway places but also trips near home. A short break in an alpine resort or by the sea can be as rewarding and exciting as a tour of the Amazonas. A car journey without a clear destination, a week on a bicycle in your own country, a few days hiking in the mountains can be adventurous and satisfying.

Nowadays we are used to flying everywhere. This is fine when one has little time, but arriving in a few hours at the destination deprives one of experiencing the journey toward it. I have always preferred to travel slowly: by train and by bus, by car, by hitchhiking, on bicycle and on foot. A worthwhile journey should not be rushed. The way is as important as the destination. Without reaching it, the traveller is still left with the memories of attempting to get there and back.

For this book I have selected the episodes of the journeys I remember best. These include holiday trips, travels I undertook in connection with my work as well as hikes and climbs in the mountains. We are not talking here about great and dangerous expeditions into the unknown, but about the kind of journeys anybody can take who wants more than sun sand and sea.

Bon voyage!

Chapter 1: First travels and early dreams

1.1 Vienna and Salzburg after World War II

I grew up in Austria in the years following the Second World War. My mother died in June 1945 from diphtheria in a camp in Bavaria a few months before the war ended. Mothers with young children had been moved there from Vienna, to escape the bombings by the Allies. My father was unable to take care of his children. My sister, Ilse, who was four years old, was taken in by our father's sister, Aunt Hanna in Vienna, and I, who was a year and a half, was raised by the brother of our deceased mother and his wife in Salzburg. There I lived with Uncle Erich and Aunt Friedl until I was ten and finished primary school. After that our father decided to look after us. My sister and I lived with him in Vienna for a few years. When I was fourteen, our father died unexpectedly. My sister was taken back by Aunt Hanna and I returned to my uncle and aunt in Salzburg.

The post war years were hard times. Austria regained her independence in 1955 and the economy was in a poor state. My foster parents had enough income to provide for the necessities of life. I was dressed and fed very well. Aunt Friedl was a good seamstress and made most of my clothes, and she was an excellent cook. Our apartment was rented, and it was in a house that dated back to the first half of the 17th century. It had been, so I was told with a certain pride, in the possession of the archbishop of Salzburg during the time of the Thirty Years War. It was spacious and comfortable. Although we lived well enough there was no money for anything beyond the essentials. My foster parents would have liked to own a car but could not afford one. They also dreamt of buying a piece of land and building their own house. Uncle Erich spent many evenings designing our future house, which never became a reality.

During the summer vacations we went either to the nearby mountains or to the lakes. Both were nearby. Salzburg is blessed with a splendid environment. It is surrounded by the Alps and the lakes of the *Salzkammergut*. My uncle was a passionate alpinist and my aunt loved the lakes. Her favorite was the *Wallersee* just half an hour's busride from Salzburg.

The first memories of travel I have are the rail journeys to the alpine town of Werfen, 30 km south of Salzburg, where we were picked up by a mule-drawn cart and transported to the Mordegg, a mountain hotel at the foothills of the mighty *Tennengebirge*. I still remember the smell of the spicy alpine air and the marvellous view from the wooden terrace across the valley to the rugged peaks of the *Steinernes Meer*. I can still see the fat cows grazing in front of the hotel.

Another early memory is that of a trip to Bad Gastein where I spent a few weeks with Aunt Hanna and Ilse. Once we went for a ride in a horse-drawn coach. I had a windmill made of paper, which I dropped from the coach. I started such a terrible row that the coachman had to stop so that my aunt could rescue the precious object. I have a vague memory of the blue walls of the hotelroom and the whistling of a train passing nearby. For a long time to come the whistling of a train would awaken in me the desire to go to faraway places. Another day we went on a chairlift. Aunt Hanna took me on her lap and I found it very exciting to see the pastures and the trees gliding by below.

Several times I travelled from Salzburg to Vienna to visit my Viennese family. I was always accompanied by an adult. Austria was then still occupied by the victorious allies. The country was divided into four zones: French, British, American and Russian. Salzburg was under American occupation. The East of Austria was controlled by the Soviets. Vienna was in the middle of the Russian zone and divided into four sectors each of which was under the rule of one of the four allies. Vienna's situation was like that of Berlin. East of Linz, at the city of Enns, the train crossed from the

American into the Russian zone. The train stopped at the checkpoint and Russian soldiers, in brown uniforms, scrutinized our passports. To this day I remember the air of fear that gripped the passengers when the Russians boarded the train. It seemed that everybody was afraid to be ordered out and God only knew what might happen then. As far as I know nothing ever happened. In fact, the Russian soldiers were mostly very friendly to me, they seemed to like children.

My father's flat in Vienna was situated in the British sector, Aunt Hanna's lived in the *Siebensterngasse* in the American sector. Opposite her apartment was a cinema, the *Kosmoskino*. American soldiers and their Austrian girl friends went there to see Hollywood films in the orginal language.

A few blocks away, as one walked along the Siebensterngasse towards the nearby city centre was an abandoned sports hall. It had played a crucial role in July 1934. A gang of Nazis assembled there before they went to the *Ballhausplatz* and assassinated the chancellor Engelbert Dollfuss. The putsch failed, however. It was to take another four years before the country fell to the German invaders. When the Nazis finally took over in 1938, they renamed the Siebensterngasse to *Straße der Julikämpfer* (Street of the Fighters of July) in memory of the members of the assassins, who were then worshipped as heroes. After the end of the war the street got its old name back.

Walking further towards the centre of Vienna, one soon enters the *Ringstrasse*, the glorious architectural monument of the reign of Emperor Franz Joseph I and from there further into the centre and into the past of Vienna: the baroque buildings, the medieval cathedral and the remnants of the Roman period. Between the *Ringstrasse* and the city centre one passes the splendid *Heldenplatz* (heroes' square) with the statues of the military leaders Prince Eugen of Savoy and Archduke Karl. On the balcony of the Imperial Palace, flanking the Heldenplatz, stood Hitler on 15th March 1938 proclaiming Austria's return into the German *Reich* in front of a huge and enthusiastic crowd.

Walking two or three kilometres one passes through many layers of Austrian and European history. Very early I learned to associate travelling with experiencing different ways of life, political situations and historic memories.

Aunt Hanna owned a weekend house in Essling, East of Vienna in the Russian sector. The journey from the Siebensterngasse to Essling was an odyssey. First we took the tramway number 49 as far as the Bellaria on the Ringstrasse. From there we continued with tram T as far as the third district to very near where my father lived. There we had to change onto number 25 that brought us as far as the Prater, Vienna's legendary fairground. We changed tram once again and passed through the village of Aspern. There stands a monument representing a lion. It commemorates the battle of Aspern in 1809, where Napoleon lost the nimbus of invincibility. Archduke Karl inflicted the first, albeit minor, defeat on the Grande Armée in the swamps near the Danube. From the final tram stop we had to walk for about twenty minutes across a Russian military airfield to the weekend house. War planes thundered above our heads as they landed and took off.

The journeys between Salzburg and Vienna were the furthest I undertook in my childhood. But, even small train journeys were an adventure. Aunt Friedl had relations in Bad Ischl whom we sometimes visited. In the early fifties we travelled by the famous *Ischler Bahn*, which was a narrow-gauge railway that had been built by Uncle Erich's father. A few years later the Ischler Bahn was dismantled in spite of heavy protests and replaced in the name of progress by a bus service. The preparations for the journey had started the day before our departure and there always seemed to be an incredible amount to be done before finally taking the tram to the railway station. We had tons of food with us as if we were to set out for an expedition into the unknown. Sometimes the preparations for these momentous journeys caused so much anxiety to my poor aunt that she woke up with a terrible headache in the morning and decided that she could not face the journey to Ischl, so that we all ended up staying at home.

1.2 Sun over the Adriatic

After finishing primary school I moved to Vienna and lived with my father and my sister in a flat beside the *Großmarkthallen*. These two enormous halls of iron structures housed an abundance of food stalls. One was the *Fleischmarkhalle* that sold meat products, the other, the *Gemüsemarkhalle*, sold fruits and vegetables. They were similar to *Les Halles* in Paris, which were known as the belly of the French capital. Neither the Großmarkthalle nor Les Halles exist any longer. Les Halles were replaced by an underground shopping and amusement complex, the Großmarkthallen had to give way to an enormous shopping mall of no architectural merit.

Our father was always short of money. He had so little that there was no point in even dreaming of buying a car or drawing designs for a future house, as Uncle Erich in Salzburg did. He had other dreams, however. He had grown up in Banja Luka and in Bosanski Novi in Bosnia where his father, my grandfather Eduard Herzmann, was head surgeon. Our mother was born in Sarajevo. She met our father in Belgrade, where she gave birth to my sister Ilse in 1941. A few days after Ilse's birth, on 27th March 1941, the Germans bombed Belgrade. Our parents fled with Ilse to Vienna, where I was born two years later.

When they lived in Yugoslavia before the war our parents spent many holidays on the Dalmation coast. Whenever our father talked about the Adriatic Sea, which is called *Adria* in German, his eyes lit up and he put all the enthusiasm of his bygone youth into the word. He extended the a-vowel thus giving it a magical sound. Very soon this caused in my sister and myself a desperate longing to see this wonderful blue *Aaadria*.

Our father often took us to the cinema. Once we saw the film *Sonne über der Adria* (Sun over the Adriatic). In one scene René

Carol, a popular German singer of that time, was sitting on a stone wall, the blue sea behind him, and accompanying himself with his guitar to a song that contained the words: *Sonne über der Adria, das ist Sonne für uns zwei…..* (The sun shining over the Adriatic is the sun for the two of us). My sister and I became determined to visit the *Adria* and pestered our father to take us there in the summer holidays instead of taking us for long walks in the Vienna Woods or for a swim in the *Alte Donau*, a still side arm of the Danube.

Ilse came up with a brilliant plan. Why not save a small amount of money, say ten *Schillinge*, every day? After a year or two this should amount to enough to pay for a family holiday in Dubrovnik or Split. Immediately this plan was put into action and every day ten Schillinge were placed into a special box which began to fill up promisingly. Unfortunately, our father was forever in financial difficulties. He owed money to many friends whom he sometimes had to pay back, there were nasty bills to be paid for such trivial things as gas and electricity and there was the rent. And on top of all this we had to eat. When a financial crisis arose, our father was forced to borrow some money from our box. He promised to repay it, but somehow this proved to be impossible. In time the box was depleted and no more money was put in. A beautiful dream had come to an end.

My longing to see *das Meer*, the sea, remained unfulfilled for some time to come. When I was fifteen – I was again living with Aunt Friedl and Uncle Erich in Salzburg after my father's death – I was determined to become a sailor. My dream was to be a captain and to travel round the world. Hamburg was *das Tor zur Welt* (the door to the world). I had read this expression somewhere, perhaps in a book by the then well known German travel writer A. E. Johann. My foster parents had given me one of his books that bore the title *Große Weltreise*: A Big Travel Round the World. On its cover was a beautiful oceanliner – this was still the time of the big steam ships. My desire to see the Adriatic Sea was replaced by an irresistable wish to visit Hamburg.

When I was sixteen I hitchhiked with my schoolmate Friedemann Bachleitner from Salzburg through Germany and Holland.
Our aim was to get to Bremen and to Hamburg, cities whose names
for me had an almost sacred aura. In Cologne on the Rhine,
Friedemann had the idea to go to the harbour and try hitch a lift
from one of the trawler ships to Rotterdam. If one can travel per
Auto-Stopp why should it not be possible to go per *Schiff-Stopp*? To
my surprise the strategy worked. The first skipper we asked was a
Dutchman who agreed to take us to Rotterdam. The journey would
take two days with one overnight on the ship. It was my first time
on a ship. It was not an ocean going ship but it was a ship and I
was in heaven. For two days and a night I was in my element as a
future captain. In Rotterdam I saw a real harbour for the very first
time in my life. The harbour of Rotterdam was then the biggest in
the world. And then, in Scheveningen, I had my first experience of
the sea stretching out into infinity. I was simply overwhelmed by
all of this.

I was impressed by the views into eternity the sea offered and I
discovered that a flat countryside, like that of Holland had its
attractions. The sunsets are wonderful and there is a sense of
expanse, which one does not get when surrounded by mountains.
However, after a few days I began to miss the mountains. I
mentioned this to a Dutchman who gave us a lift in his car. He told
me that when he was in Innsbruck he missed the views into the
distance. He felt hemmed in by the mountains. I never felt hemmed
in by mountains. They were there to be summited! From the top of
a mountain one could see even further than when standing on a
Dutch plain.

All these sensations, impressions and experiences made me
aware of my dependence on nature for my emotional wellbeing.
For the past forty years I have lived in Ireland surrounded by the
sea. I love the sea, but when I am back in Austria I do not miss it.
However, I seek out the mountains wherever I am. I hike regularly
in the Dublin and Wicklow Mountains, on the doorstep of the city,
but I really love the mountains of Connemara and Kerry, in the

West and Southwest of the island, for their alpine flair. The Maam Turks and the Twelve Bens remind me very much of the Tennengebirge where Uncle Erich brought me hiking with his schnautzer dog Puck. I am most happy in landscapes where there are mountains. I have not become a sailor.

A good few more years had to pass before I finally saw the *Adria*. I was studying German Literature and History at the University of Vienna when I fell in love with an American girl, who spent a year in Austria, in order to learn German. She was a student of Art History and it was a requirement, imposed by her course directors, that she would learn that language. Ann's field was Byzantine Art and the University of Vienna had an internationally renowned Byzantinist, Otto Demus, under whom she hoped to study. Her parents had bought her a Volkswagen. With this small vehicle we undertook an epic journey, in the summer of 1966, to what was then still Yugoslavia. We spent two weeks in Serbia, Kosovo and Macedonia in search of Byzantine monasteries with their fabulous fresco paintings of the 13th and 14th centuries. It was a wonderful world which I had known nothing of until then. And it was in that summer that I saw for the first time the *Aaadria* I had longed to see for so many years.

To this day the Dalmation coast to me is the most beautiful coast in the world. It is a rocky coast with the mountains rising steeply up to one side of the road. There are innumerable little inlets with small and pebbly beaches. Often one has to climb down to them with difficulty and then plunge into the water from some rockface. More than thousand islands line the coast.

But not only nature offers stunning sights. The cities are equally beautiful. There is the medieval gem of Zadar, the Roman city of Split with the palace of Diocletian and the wonder of the sea, Dubrovnik, founded by the Venetians. My father had often mentioned Dubrovnik. However, he did not call it by that name but by its former name *Ragusa*. Pronouncing Ragusa he lengthened the u vowel in a fashion similar to the one he extended the a in

Adria, in this endowing the name of this city with all his *Heimweh* and *Fernweh*.

The North Sea had impressed me very much a few years earlier, but the Adriatic Sea was what I really had been looking for. It may well have been that being in love added to my emotional high. Be that as it may, all the dreams of my youth, my romantic *Fernweh* and *Wanderlust* found complete fulfilment.

Chapter 2: Switzerland and France by bicycle 1962

2.1 The Way from Salzburg to Paris

I love cities. Whenever I visited my aunts in Vienna in the 1950s and early 1960s I was fascinated by the historical layers one could walk through in a very short time. The great cities of Europe are preserving our history in stone and brick, in paintings, institutions, and customs etc. In Vienna one finds Europe's history compressed into a few square miles. With her glorious architecture, Vienna is also very pleasing to the eye. So are other European capital cities, most of all Paris. Apart from dreaming of the *Adria* I had always wanted to see the *City of Light*. After finishing high school I did not want to wait any longer. Since I had nobody to accompany me, I decided to cycle from Salzburg to Paris on my own.

I left Salzburg at the beginning of July. Cycling through the Tyrol and Vorarlberg was tough as I had to cross the Arlberg Mountain Pass. It took me a few days to get to the Swiss border. My first destination was Dornach near Basel. There was (and still is) the *Goetheanum*, the world centre of anthroposophy. A school friend, Mario, was an anthroposopher and had a summer job in the Goetheanum. He had said I could stop in Dornach en route to Paris, work in the Goetheanum for some time and earn money for the continuation of my journey.

Before I arrived in Dornach I knew nothing about anthroposophy. During my stay I learned that the Waldorf schools were run by the anthoposophic movement on anti-authoritarian and holistic principles, that anthroposophy favoured organic farming or biodynamic agriculture, that there was an alternative anthroposophic medicine that treated not only the physical side of the illness but considered the patient as a totality of mind and body. There also was an anthroposphic architecture of which the Goetheanum was a prime example. It influenced some important architects of the 20th century such as Richard Neutra, Le Corbusier, Henry van de Velde, Eero Saarinen, Frank Lloyd Wright, Erich

Mendelsohn and Hans Scharoun. The founder of the movement was the Austrian philosopher Rudolf Steiner (1861 – 1925).

Mario introduced me to Mr. K, who was the head of the cleaning brigade and who agreed to take me on. He was a short, slim man who permanently had a thick cigar in his mouth. He ran the cleaning of the Goetheanum like a military operation. The cleaners were paid according to how many hours they spent on their knees scrubbing the floors of the innumerable rooms. Hard working cleaners were rewarded with lots of cleaning time and thus given the opportunity to earn good money. Lazy cleaners got less work and thus less pay.

Every day Mr Kumm made a delicious muesli. He put sour milk, fruit, nuts and oats into a big open barrel and stirred the mixture while holding his burning cigar in his mouth. If a bit of ash was added to the mush it did no harm. Whenever we felt like it we dipped our mugs and spoons into this mixture. All modern day rules of hygiene were completely ignored. Mr K's muesli tasted out of this world. Never again have I tasted one like it.

The cleaners were accommodated in the boiler house whose chimney stack was shaped like a flame. We slept there and we had a kitchen where we could cook our meals. There were about ten cleaners, all in their late teens and early twenties and of many different nationalities. A Dutch guy called Theo did most of the cooking. He was a good cook unhampered by worry about health and safety. He wore an apron that was never washed and he used the same cloth for mopping up the floor and drying the dishes. Nobody ever got ill.

All the anthroposphers I met in the Goetheanum were lovely people. They displayed a gentle and tolerant nature and were committed pacifists. Most of them were spending a few weeks there to take part in courses or attend concerts, theatre performances and lectures. Once I attended a concert. A string quartet by Mozart was performed and simultaneously translated into movements by a dance ensemble. The holistic world view held that everything is connected to everything. Thus, for example, the musical movements had their counterpart in the movements of the body.

On another day I saw a performance of *Alexanders Wandlung*, a play written in 1953 by Albert Steffen, who after the death of Rudolf Steiner in 1925 became president of the Anthroposophical Society. It is a very long four-act play of which I did not understand a word. Later I read that the play depicts the journey of Alexander the Great, after his death, through the regions of the spirit till his return to earth. Parallel to Alexander's journey through these higher regions we are shown the ever changing events on earth. What made an impression on me was the way the actors spoke. They did not speak "normally" nor in a manner in which actors emphazise the lines of elevated prose in classical drama. What I heard was something between the spoken and the sung word. But it was not *recitative* either. Some vowels were lengthened inordinately, important passages were cited in higher pitch, others in lower pitch, some loud, some almost inaudible. Language was not just language as we normally use it. It was an expressive (or expressionist) language of music, rhythm, emotion and movement. I was told that on certain occasions Goethe's complete *Faust* was performed in this way.

One day I was cheerfully cleaning away while whistling the tune of Papageno's song *Der Vogelfänger bin ich ja* of Mozart's *Magic Flute*. I was approaching a corner and stopped whistling because I had run out of breath. Next moment I heard someone round the corner taking up the tune. It was Tony, an English student who was there with his friend Phil, also from England. Their plan was to get to Salzburg and attend some of the performances at the Salzburg Festival. They had stopped over in the Goetheanum in order to earn enough money so that they could carry on with their journey. As Tony and Phil were not very hard workers Mr K had little time for them and thus gave them little work. He always referred to them as *die Tommies*. As a consequence they did not earn enough money to go to Salzburg. Although their work ethos may not have been up to Swiss standards, Tony and Phil were lovely fellows and we became good friends. They were students of history and on the path of becoming teachers.

The following year Tony travelled to Salzburg and spent part of the summer holidays with me, (or rather with Aunt Friedl and Uncle Erich). In the same summer I went with him to England and spent the rest of the holidays with his parents in Littleport near Ely. Tony was very interested in local history. He knew a lot about Ely Cathedral and could show me parts of that wonderful building that were not normally open to the public.

Travelling between Britain and Central Europe was cumbersome compared to today. Those were the times before cheap flights. England and Austria were connected by rail and ferry. As students we could avail of reduced fares through the Anglo-Austrian society. It took two days to get from Austria to England. I lost contact with Phil after a while, but Tony became a lifelong friend.

2.2 The way back

I had another experience on my way back from Paris that made a lasting impression on me. After a day of cycling away from Paris in an easterly direction I came to Fère Champenoise, a small village in the Marne region. As night was approaching I looked for a place to stay. No hotel or hostel was anywhere in sight. In my poor French I asked a woman who was passing by if she might know where I could stay. She very kindly offered me a place in her house. Because of my poor language skills we could not strike up a lively conversation as we walked to her house. After a few minutes of silence she asked me where I was from. When I said *Autriche* her eyes lit up and she exclaimed: *Ah, Österreich, ich bin aus der Tschechoslovakei!* She was Czech by birth, spoke good German and was pleased to meet somebody from a country that shared so much history with her own. She treated me with the same enthusiasm as she would have treated a Czech compatriot. Her husband was

French and they lived in a very comfortable house. I was given a great dinner with wine, a room for the night and a good breakfast. Madame D told me that she owned a small flat in Neuilly sur Seine very near Paris and that I would be welcome to stay there if I wanted to return in the future. When I left in the morning, she gave me home made *Powidltascherl*, a Czech-Austrian sweet speciality, and a bottle of wine for the journey.

I stayed in contact with Madame D for some time. When after a few years I thought of visiting Paris again, I wrote to her and asked if her offer still stood. A letter came back from her husband telling me the shocking news that a few months earlier my kind hostess had been hit by a car outside her house and died.

My time in Paris fell between these two unforgettable events. Paris had been my destination, but my memories of this wonderful city are vague. However, I remember vividly my time in the Goetheanum and the beginning of my friendship with Tony that ended only a few years ago when he died. And the kind Madame D will always live in my memory. The way to Paris and the way back home left a deeper impression than Paris itself.

There is no need to describe that city and praise her cultural monuments and her wonderful urban flair. I visited as many of the famous sights as I could pack in with the result that my memory of what I saw is somewhat blurred. I stayed in a hostel run by UNESCO. We got a breakfast of *café au lait* and a baguette with butter. As money was tight I used public transport sparingly, instead, I cycled and walked a lot. I often had to ask for directions, which gave me the opportunity to practice the little French I had. Contrary to what many travellers say about the Parisians, I found them extremely friendly and charming. Sometimes I teamed up for my sightseeing tours with other guests of the hostel. I remember a young man from India who wanted to know what constituted the difference between a Romanesque building and one from the high middle ages. I was always hungry, as all I could afford was hot dogs and pommes frites. No wonder that after a week I was totally exhausted and felt that it was time to start the arduous journey back home.

I had planned to visit Versailles but lacked the energy to do so. My lovely Czech hostess in Fère Champenoise expressed great surprise when I told her that I had not seen Louis' XIV architectural extravaganza: *What, you have been to Paris and you have not seen Versailles?!* Perhaps this was the reason she offered me her apartment in Paris. Many years later I visited Paris with Ursula. It was November and we took the train to Versailles where we got a guided tour in English. The guide was excellent and we were only five people in the group. What a privilege it was to get a tour of that palace through which thousands of tourists are normally pushed every day!

After leaving Madam D it took me two days to reach Strassburg and there my resolve to carry on left me. I went to the railway station and found out that a train to Salzburg was leaving in the morning. After spending the night on a bench outside the station I boarded the train. Thus ended my first journey to the City of Light.

Chapter 3: Yugoslavia 1966 – 2007

3.1 A vanished country

All through my childhood Yugoslavia to me was first and foremost the country by the Adriatic Sea. My parents and grandparents on my father's and mother's side had lived there before I was born. My father's father was a surgeon in Bosanski Novi (today Novi Grad) near Sarajevo, which was part of the Austro-Hungarian Monarchy till the end of the First World War. My father, my mother and Aunt Hanna were born in Bosnia. After 1918 the different countries and regions of the Southern Slavs united and formed the Kingdom of Yugoslavia. The new state consisted of what today are Bosnia, Slovenia, Croatia, Macedonia, Kosovo, Montenegro and Serbia. Up until 1918 Bosnia, Slovenia, Croatia and a part of Serbia were part of Austria-Hungary.

After the collapse of the Habsburg Monarchy my grandparents and my parents stayed in the new country and became Yugoslavs. They belonged to the German-speaking minority of the Yugoslavian kingdom and their identity was somewhat confused. Although they felt close to the culture of the German speaking countries, they had a strong sense of loyalty to the Serbian royal house. They all spoke German and Serbo-Croat with equal fluency. My sister was born in Belgrade. When the Nazis bombed the city in April 1941, my parents moved to Vienna where they felt safer. I was born there two years later. After my mother's death my father settled in Vienna. He became an Austrian citizen but never a good Austrian. For the rest of his life, he was homesick for Yugoslavia and the Dalmatian coast. On Sundays he sometimes attended the services in the Serbian Orthodox Church in Vienna's 3RD district, where he mingled with the Serb expats and conversed with them in their language.

After the Second World War the Kingdom of Yugoslavia was no more. It had been replaced by Tito's Communist regime. Nevertheless, as an ideal and as a physical entity Yugoslavia still was the home of all Southern Slavs and Albanians as well as of Catholic and Orthodox Christians and of Muslims. It could be said that Yugoslavia was the true successor of the multi-national and multi-ethnic Habsburg Empire and that like the Austro-Hungarian Monarchy it was doomed to fail once nationalism became rampant. While the Habsburg Empire had held together for hundreds of years and managed to withstand the nationalist onslaught of the 19th century until 1918, communist Yugoslavia fell victim to a wave of a vicious new nationalism only a few years after Tito's death.

I was lucky to visit Tito's Yugoslavia a few times when it still appeared to be a credible alternative to the Soviet Communist model and an example of the viability of a multi-national, multi-ethnic and multi-cultural state. Unlike my parents, my mother's sister Aunt Gerda and her Serb husband Vojeslav (Vojo) had not fled from Belgrade when the Nazis bombed it. They had two children: a daughter, Dušanka and a son, Dejan.

In 1960, when still in high school, Ilse and I were invited to spend a few weeks of the summer holidays in Belgrade. Aunt Gerda and Uncle Vojo spoke perfect German, our cousins Dejan and Dušanka , however, did not. After the war, so I was told, it had not been advisable to be heard speaking German anywhere in Belgrade, therefore my aunt and uncle decided not to teach their children the language of the hated enemy in order to avoid hostilities and possible discrimination. Our cousins and Ilse had French, and I spoke some English. But we all learned Latin in school. So, we communicated through this ancient *lingua franca*. Initially, it was not easy but it certainly was fun. We got better with practice and after a few days we even managed to tell jokes!

I then knew very little about the history and the political situation of Yugoslavia. Belgrade to me was a somewhat exotic city, but not that exotic that I did not feel at home after a few days. I liked the buzz of the place, the restaurants by the riverside, the spicy food and the open-air markets. It was a bit run down, but Vienna, and most European cities at that time were no different. In spite of the grey and shabby facades of the houses, Belgrade gave the impression of being a vibrant place.

Uncle Vojo was a staunch anti-communist and made no secret of it. One day a friend of his offered to take us for a drive to the surroundings of the city. Uncle Vojo warned me that his friend was a supporter of Tito and that I should refrain from making any derogatory remarks about the regime. In spite of their political differences my uncle and his communist friend got on very well. However, when he found it necessary, Uncle Vojo could stand up fearlessly to the authorities of Tito's state. One day we were walking in a park and observed a policeman, showing a boy how to use a Flobert gun to shoot birds. My uncle was outraged. He told off the policeman most severely for teaching a boy to kill innocent birds and by doing so endangering passers-by. My uncle's angry tirades made the policeman shrink by a size or two and in the end the poor guardian of the peace ended up apologizing profusely.

During my first visit to Yugoslavia I did not see the Adriatic sea. I had to wait another six years. The opportunity arose in the summer of 1966 when I met Ann. She was a great admirer of Byzantine Art and knew a lot about it. Together we visited the medieval Serbian Orthodox monasteries that were famous for their frescoes. Whereas the Byzantine monasteries and churches in Italy and Greece (Palermo, Monreale, Ravenna, Thessaloniki and others) are known for their mosaics, the Serbian kings after winning independence from the Byzantine Empire employed painters to decorate their churches. They left Serbia with a unique heritage.

One finds rudiments of medieval Byzantine frescoes in other parts of the world, for example in Pürgg and in Lambach, both in Austria. What makes the Serbian monasteries so special is that the frescoes of their churches cover all the walls and ceilings and amount to a carefully planned iconographic programme. In the apse one normally finds the twelve apostles, above them is Mary, the four corners of the cupola depict the symbols of the four evangelists, bull, eagle, man and lion. In the cupola is Christ the Redeemer. The walls of the naves are covered with juxtaposed scenes of the Old and New Testaments. For example, on the wall opposite the resurrection of Christ, we may see Jonah in the belly of the whale. Jonah spent three days inside the whale and then returned to life outside. This story from the Old Testament was understood to anticipate Christ's three days in the tomb and his following resurrection. Sometimes there is room for scenes depicting the lives of Saints and even of Serbian kings and queens. A fresco showing the death of a Serbian queen may closely follow the iconography of the Death of Mary on the opposite wall. Obviously, that was not considered blasphemous.

The best known of these monastic gems are Mileševa near Prijepolje, Dečani near Peć, two churches in Peć, Gračanica near Priština, Sopoćani near Novi Pazar and Studenica a bit further north of Novi Pazar. While Mileševa, Sopoćani and Studenica are today still in Serbia, Dečani and the churches in Peć as well as Gračanica, are now in the newly established state of Kosovo. This is particularly hurtful to the Serbs as these monasteries are an essential part of Serbian history and cultural heritage. Peć used to be the seat of the Patriarch of the Serbian Orthodox Church. It is as if Lower Austria had lost the monasteries of Klosterneuburg, Göttweig, Dürnstein and Melk to a new hostile state, or England had been forced to hand over the regions that locate the Cathedrals of Canterbury, Ely, Wells or Winchester to an enemy.

As I had not yet learned to drive, Ann took it upon herself to drive all the way. It was an epic journey lasting about four weeks. She planned the route in such a way that we would take in as many Byzantine sights as possible. In 1966 Yugoslavia still existed. Kosovo was part of it, so were Bosnia, Croatia and Slovenia. We moved through Slovenia to Rijeka, drove alongside the coast to Zadar and Dubrovnik, then to Mostar and Sarajevo and then turning east to Kraljevo. After that we turned south again to Novi Pazar, taking in the monasteries of Studenica and Milešiva, and continued further south to Peć, Dečani and Prizren. We drove as far as

Skopje and from there to Lake Ochrid near the Albanian border. Turning north again we visited Gračanica and Priština and finally arrived in Belgrade. We visited Uncle Vojo and my cousins who still lived in the same apartment where I had stayed six years previously. Aunt Gerda had died a few years earlier. From Belgrade we drove on the *autoput* (a kind of motorway without a barrier separating the oncoming traffic) direction West to Zagreb and back to Austria.

When travelling in Yugoslavia, we encountered no borders. In each region we met people with different religions, different customs, music and folklore, but everybody was Yugoslav. How different this is today! There are borders everywhere. Slovenia and Croatia are now members of the EU, the other successor states of Yugoslavia are still on the waiting list and may remain there for a long time. Apart from the Slovenes everybody spoke the same language, Serbo-Croatian. True, the Croatians as Catholics use Latin letters, the Orthodox Serbs and Montenegrins write in Cyrillic letters. But it was considered to be one language and people understood each other perfectly. Now the Serbs speak Serbian, the Bosnians Bosnian, the Macedonians Macedonian, the Montenegrins Montenegrin and the Croats Croatian. Should the Serbs and the Bosnians and Montenegrins join the EU, they and the Croats will probably insist that all documents are translated into their now different languages. The Croats will pretend that they do not understand Serbian and vice versa, the Bosnians will claim that they are unable to read documents in Serbian or Montenegrin and so on. It is like if the Chileans insisted on translations of Spanish into Chilean, the Peruvians asking for translations of anything written in Ecuadorian, or if the Austrians asked for translations of texts written by their German neighbours. The Bible tells us that Babel caused a great confusion, because all of a sudden everybody spoke a different language. The successor states of Yugoslavia are trying hard to recreate Babel.

3.2 Novi Pazar and the Adriatic coast

We arrived in Novi Pazar on the evening of 9th September 1966. En route from Kraljevo we had visited the stunning monasteries of Žiča and Studenica. On the following day we planned to see Sopoćani and Mileševa and then continue our journey to Peć. Impressive as all these sacred sites with their byzantine frescoes were, Novi Pazar as it was then presented itself to us in a wonderfully exotic light. It is located in what under Turkish rule was called the Sandžak region, and when we arrived there, we felt we had left Europe, gone back in time and entered the Ottoman Empire. There were old Turkish houses and mosques and Orthodox churches. The streets were crowded with people and there were almost no cars. In the centre of the town we spotted a brand-new hotel on the main square. It was the only Western style building to be seen. Assuming that this was where we had to stay, Ann parked the car and I got out and walked to the hotel with the intention of asking for a room for one night. It was closed. There was no notice indicating when, or if, it would open.

When I walked back, the car was surrounded by a hundred or more people who stared in awe at the black Volkswagen with a foreign registration and at the driver inside who did not know where to look in order to conceal her embarrassment. When I approached, the crowd stood back very politely and opened a passage for me. We then discovered an old Turkish style building on the other side of the square that appeared to be a hotel of a more traditional kind. We had no problem getting a room there. The accommodation was basic. As it was very hot, we had to leave the window facing the square open. There was shouting and music all night and we did not sleep a wink.

After checking in, we strolled around the town looking for a place where we could eat. The news that strangers had come to town had spread like wildfire. Many people approached us, chatting us up, asking us questions about ourselves or offering help. We ended in the company of a few young men who turned out to be very kind guides. They were happy to practice a bit of English and German, so communication was all right. One of the men had been a Serb lightweight boxing champion who had given up the sport after he was defeated and injured. We ate some *ćevapčići* with delicious freshly baked white bread and our hosts insisted on buying us beer and *šljvovica*. They did not expect anything in return. What they offered was pure unselfish hospitality, for which the Slavs, especially the Serbs, are well known.

I returned to Novi Pazar many years later when I revisited Yugoslavia with Ursula in 1990. We drove to Belgrade and stayed with Uncle Vojo and my cousin Dušanka, who had married Danilo, a man from Montenegto. They had two children, Jelena and Blagoje. We then drove south, as I wanted to show Ursula the Serbian monasteries. Dušanka, Jelena and Blagoe accompanied us. We drove in two cars as Dušanka and her children had to go back to Belgrade while Ursula and I planned to drive on to Buljarica on the Adriatic Coast and from there, via the Dalmatian coast back to Ljubljana and then on to Dublin.

Dušanka had booked us into a B&B in Novi Pazar. We were to go to the hotel in the centre and phone the owner of the B&B from there. He would meet us there and bring us to his house. The hotel was oversized, empty of guests and its interior was kind of reminiscent of the Alhambra in Granada. I think it was the same hotel where Ann and I had unsuccessfully tried to get a room twenty-four years earlier. The reception was on the first floor. Above it was a big NO SMOKING sign. The two attractive and heavily made up women behind the desk were smoking. They rang our host. After waiting a few minutes, we heard the lift coming up to our floor. It stopped and somebody tried to get out. Apparently, the door was jammed and the person inside the lift started banging with his fist and then pushing against it. After a few heavy pushes the door suddenly opened and a heavily built man burst into the reception room and almost fell to the ground. He was our host, Rešad.

We did not take the hotel lift to get to the ground floor. Rešad brought us to his house in a lane called Osmana đikića. We spent two days there. It was a comfortable place and Muradija, Rešad's wife, did everything to make us feel at home. Her breakfasts were wonderful. One of her delights were *uštipci*, a kind of donut similar to the *churros* I remembered from my visits to Granada. The best way of eating them is to dip them into hot chocolate. The Spanish probably got the recipe from the Moors and the Serbs took it from the Turks.

Rešad did nothing. Whenever we passed through the living room going out in the morning and returning in the evening, he was lying on the sofa. To us he embodied what we imagined to be a pasha. He was very interested in our wellbeing. He had a little knowledge of German and kept asking how we were: *Gut schlafen? Gut essen? Gut einkaufen?*

Although the house we were staying in lived up to my expectations, I could not help being disappointed with Novi Pazar. Many of the old Turkish houses had been replaced by boring apartment blocks, few women wore the traditional clothes, most of the younger ones preferred to wear jeans. The calls for prayer sounding from the mosques were recordings. It was difficult to find a traditional bakery, where we could buy the delicious white bread I remembered. Gone was the feeling of being in the world of the Arabian Nights that I had enjoyed so much a quarter of a century earlier. Time had moved on. Novi Pazar was trying her best to become like any other place in the globalised world. Confronting the dreams of the past with the reality of the present more often than not leads to disappointment.

Yet, underneath these rather desperate attempts to catch up with globalisation, some things had not really changed. Behind the façade of modernity old attitudes persisted. We went to the post office in Novi Pazar to buy stamps. The door was closed. A hand-written sign said PAUSE. We waited for ten minutes or so and nothing happened. Finally, we gave up. We came across such

PAUSE signs many times. Whenever it suited them, the employees of banks, post offices or shops would take a break, as long as they wished. Another time we went to a bank to change money. In front of us was a family or a clan of six or more people who at the same time wanted to change German marks into dinar and put money into their saving accounts. They occupied the only two counters available. There was a lot of gesticulating and shouting and the clerks were overwhelmed. It was chaos, pure and simple. I cannot remember if we had the patience to wait until they had solved their problems.

The Serbian monasteries were as glorious as ever. I had brought a good camera and a tripod and took plenty of photographs of the frescoes. This is not always allowed. In Mileševa the frescoes were in the process of being restored under the guidance of a woman art conservator-restorer from Belgrade. She kindly allowed me to set up my tripod and take pictures. In Studenica I defied the notices saying that no pictures must be taken. There was nobody around and I worked away quite happily until an orthodox monk appeared. He looked at me and I looked at him a bit sheepish. He asked if I was *Frances*. I thought it best to pretend to be French and nodded. He seemed to be pleased and gave me a friendly slap on my shoulder and walked away. In Dečani we met a monk by name of Boreslav who told us a little about the history of the monastery. His historic reminiscences consisted mostly of the cruelties the Turks had committed in the past. If he is still alive, Boreslav will not be happy about the fact that Dečani, like the churches in Peć, as well as the monastery of Gračanica, now belong to the new nation state of Kosovo whose inhabitant are mostly Muslims.

1990 was the last year of Yugoslavia's existence. In the following year the war broke out and destroyed the country. The tensions could already be felt everywhere. We were the only tourists. Dušanka was worried about the safety of herself and her children as her car had a Belgrade (i.e. Serbian) registration. She felt safe enough in Novi Pazar because it was part of Serbia. Kosovo, however, was different. The post office in Peć was burned down. There were endless queues outside every telephone box. The rubbish had not been collected for weeks and was piling up in the streets. Serbian tanks and soldiers patrolled the streets. Nowhere did we see women driving. In the restaurants and cafes they were conspicuous by their absence. The pedestrians paid no attention to traffic lights and cars. They crossed the streets whenever it suited them. Neither did the drivers care about pedestrians. One had the sense that law and order was breaking down and that the region was in social and psychological reverse gear. Women did not seem to count. Dušanka in her Yugo Fiat was the only female driver to be seen, or shall I say: to be ignored. While she was waiting in line at a petrol station a male driver brutally forced his lorry in front her. I wonder what the situation of women now is in this new independent state of Kosovo.

After Dušanka, Jelena and Blagoe had left in order to return to Belgrade, Ursula and I travelled south to the coast. Now it was Ursula's first time to see the wonderful *Aaadria*! Near Dubrovnik in a small town called Plat we found a very attractive B&B. The house was situated about twenty metres above a strand. We took our breakfast on the terrace with a view of the sea, and one day the landlady brought us homemade apple cake to our room. From the house a few steps led down to the beach. There were safe places to swim and there was a restaurant that served freshly fried fish, squid and salads as well as rice and pasta dishes. The owner had a little terrier whose job it was to chase away feral cats. In the evenings we sat outside having our simple and delicious meals and drinking Dalmatian wine. There were very few guests. One evening the only other customers were an Irish garda (policeman) and his girlfriend. They had come all the way from Ireland on their motorbike. The air was balmy, and the moon poured her silver rays on the calm sea. It was the perfect scene for the cover of a glossy travel brochure.

3.3 Mostar 1966, 1990 and 2001

After enjoying this idyllic life for a few days, it was time to start the journey home. Our route was from Dubrovnik to Neum, Mostar, Sarajevo, Banja Luka and Zagreb to Ljubljana where we put the car on a train to Oostende. From there it was not too far back to Ireland: only two car-ferries and a 600 km drive from the east coast of England to the west coast.

At Neum we turned inland. After leaving Počitelj, where we had visited the Turkish fortress, a bus overtook us on a dangerous bend. We stopped for a picnic and then continued driving towards Mostar. Suddenly we came across a horrific scene. The bus that had overtaken us earlier had collided head on with a lorry. Bodies and pieces of luggage were scattered all over the place, police, ambulances and fire brigades were there. With great difficulty we got past the accident scene and continued our journey in a shaken state.

When I visited Mostar for the first time in 1966 with Ann, I instantly liked this old Bosnian town in the mountains, some 140 km south of Sarajevo. The fact that our hotel was very near the railway station and that we were kept awake by the constant noise and, worse, by the emissions of the steam locomotives, did not take away from the good memories I have. After Novi Pazar Mostar seemed to me to be the most "Turkish" of all places in Yugoslavia, even more so than Sarajevo.

The best-known feature of the town was the old bridge over the Neretva River. This spectacular single span stone arch bridge was almost twenty-nine metres long and twenty metres high. Mimar Hayruddin, a student of the great Ottoman architect Sinan built it in 1566. The Sultan threatened to execute Hayruddin if the bridge collapsed after the removal of the wooden supports. Legend has it that Hayruddin dug his own grave just in case. However, the bridge survived more than four hundred years. Local male youths used to show off by diving from the bridge into the river. In 1993 the bridge collapsed after Croat artillery had shelled it. When the war ended, a provisional bridge was built that connected the eastern and western parts of the town. Later Mimar Hayruddin's bridge was reconstructed with international help, and using the original plans that have been kept in an archive in Istanbul.

The visit in 1990 to Mostar was my second one. For Ursula it was the first. We arrived there later than we had planned and were short of time because we wanted to get to Banja Luka before dark. I was eager to show Ursula the famous bridge and stopped the car at a point from where we had a good view. A man approached us and offered to give us a tour of the town. He told us that he was a historian, and from what we could gather he appeared to be genuinely knowledgeable. When we explained to him that we did not have much time he promised to make the tour a short one. After some hesitation we decided that we could not delay any further as we did not wish to continue our drive on the mountainous road to Banja Luka in the dark. He was deeply offended when we left him standing there. For a long time, we felt guilty and often thought about him wondering if and how he survived the years after our brief encounter. We also wondered how our pasha in Novi Pazar and his wife had been coping with the bloody war. We will never know.

Driving towards Banja Luka we noticed that many place names were blackened out and had SDS written over them. SDS stands for *Srpska Demokratska Stranka* (Serb Democratic Party), which was founded by Jovan Rašković on 17th February 1990. Its aim was to defend Serbian national interests against the rising Croatian nationalism. In the ensuing war the SDS became the driving force behind the establishment of a Serb nationalist movement in Bosnia-Herzegovina, and it was later held responsible for many war crimes, notably for the massacre in Srebrenica. One of the most notorious leaders of that party was Radovan Karadžić. The break-up of Yugoslavia was already anticipated and the different parties were getting ready to secure as many of the spoils of the future war as possible. The aim of the SDS was to unite the Bosnian Serbs with the Serb motherland, something that was not achieved in the end.

Today Banja Luka is the de facto capital of the *Republica Srpska*, which is now an autonomous region within the independent state of Bosnia-Herzegovina.

Our hotel in Banja Luka had two beds. One was unusable because it was like a slide. Apart from the beds there was nothing in the room. A door led to a balcony without railings. Its main function was that of an ashtray. In the bar below us people kept us awake by singing in perfect harmony until one o'clock in the morning.

Eleven years later, in June 2001, Ursula and I returned to what had once been Yugoslavia. The war had ended only a short time before. Croatia, Serbia and Bosnia were now independent countries. We took a Croatian Airlines charter flight from Dublin to Split and Dubrovnik. Most passengers on the plane were pilgrims, who flew to Split from where they were transferred to Medjugorje. Only a few passengers continued on to Dubrovnik. Leaving the bus that had brought us from Dubrovnik to nearby Plat we got a shock. There were rows of buildings that had suffered badly from artillery fire. Some houses had been reduced to rubble. Others were still standing with broken windows and damaged facades.

Our hotel, however, was in perfect condition. Once we learned to ignore the sad immediate surroundings, we had a good time there. Very near the hotel was the B&B where we had stayed in 1991. The little restaurant by the beach, of which we had such romantic memories, was also still there. The little terrier, however, that used to chase away the feral cats was missing. The owner told us that the dog had been shot dead by the Serbs.

After a few days lying by the hotel pool and occasionally diving into the sea we rented a car and drove to Mostar. We were keen to see how that town was coping with the new situation. Arriving there we got another shock to see so many houses damaged or destroyed. The Neretva River divides the city. The Catholic Croats live east of the river, the Muslim quarters are on the east side. We got the definite impression that the Croats were unhappy to live in a state and in a town they had to share with the (Muslim) Bosnians. All over the Croatian side we saw Croatian flags and Christian crosses. All the shops and restaurants accepted the Croatian kuna.

We crossed the provisional bridge that was erected after Mimar Hayruddin's masterpiece had been destroyed by the Croats and sat down in a café. When it came to paying the waitress refused to accept Croatian money. Bosnia had the Bosnian Mark and this was the only currency with which one could pay in this part of the town. The waitress told us off in good German: "if you visit a foreign country you pay in the currency of the country", full stop. We tried to explain to her that we were, of course, aware of that but that we had been told before coming here that the kuna was accepted anywhere in Bosnia. What we not had been told was how intensive the hostility between Croats and Bosnians (or Catholics and Muslims) still was. We should have known better.

3.4 Slavonic hospitality

The hospitality that we experienced in Novi Pazar in 1966 is not unusual in Serbia. Serbian hospitality is a serious matter. How serious it was I learned in 2007 when Ursula and I visited my Serb relations in Belgrade. Dušanka's and Danilo's children, Blagoje and Jelena, had grown into young adults. Also present was my cousin Dejan who had married a Dutchwomen, Maret. They lived in Amsterdam but spent a lot of their time in Belgrade. One day Dejan rented a bus and drove us into the surroundings of the Serb capital. Somewhere in a remote place we stopped at a restaurant where a suckling pig was roasting on a spit. Sitting in the open air, we ate the meat, salads and white bread. It was delicious. We knew that Danilo and Dejan would foot the bill, but Ursula thought that it might be a good idea if we paid as we had availed of the hospitality of my Serb cousins for a few days. So, I sneaked off and settled the bill behind the backs of Dejan and Danilo. When they found out they were deeply offended. I had disregarded Serbian hospitality! I don't think they ever forgave me.

Twenty years earlier, in 1967, I had experienced another feast of Slavonic hospitality, that time not in Serbia, but in Bulgaria. One year after our visit to the Serbian monasteries, Ann decided to undertake another epic journey to Bulgaria and Greece in search of further Byzantine treasures. Once again, I accompanied her. 1967 was the first year when Bulgaria had abolished many of the restrictions Western tourists had to face when visiting that country. Now one could easily get a visa at the border. It was valid for one month and travel by car was completely unrestricted. B&Bs were readily available everywhere. When driving into a town or city there was normally a tourist office where you could book private accommodation.

Driving through Bulgaria was sheer pleasure. Traffic was sparse, most roads, even the main roads, were paved with cobblestones. The countryside looked very well cared for. The crops were automatically irrigated and there were many people working in the fields, most of them women. They waved at us as we drove by. It felt like being in a kitschy *Heimatfilm*. If someone had painted the scene (strong and healthy-looking women working in beautiful fields and happily waving at cars driving by), the result would have been a perfect example of Soviet social-realist art, propagating the benefits of the communist system.

The Bulgarians not only waved at us as we drove by them. Whenever we stopped in a village our car was immediately surrounded by a crowd, we were invited into houses, offered coffee and shown places they thought might be of interest to us. It was sometimes difficult to stick to our travel timetable as the hospitable locals refused to let us go. Even if a lot of this hospitality may have been motivated by curiosity about Westerners it was still remarkable. When a few weeks later we crossed the Turkish border and arrived in Edirne, the contrast to Bulgaria could not be greater. Some street urchins approached us and tried to sell us postcards. We declined politely. As we walked on, they pelted us with stones.

Ann had brought a book with her, by David Rice, on Byzantine Art that listed the churches with the frescoes she wanted to see. We often asked passers-by how to get to this or that church. As we spoke no Bulgarian, we used sign language and when that failed Ann took out her sketchbook and made a little drawing. If, for example, we were looking for the church of the Archangel Gabriel, Ann drew the outlines of a byzantine church (layout like a Greek cross, cupola in the middle), beside it a figure of an archangel, (a creature with two very long wings), and wrote "Gabriel" beside it. The interesting thing was that the men we asked never knew what we meant while the women understood immediately.

David Rice's book mentioned frescoes in a church high in the mountains, near a remote little town whose name and location I have forgotten. Ann was determined to find the church and the frescoes. We arrived in the town in the late morning and went into the post office hoping that somebody there could tell us how to get there. The two ladies behind the counter spoke a little French and German and they knew where the church was, but told us that it would be difficult for us to find it. They offered to be our guides. Before closing the post office, they rang a doctor in the hospital and asked him if he would join us. The good doctor had to decline as he was scheduled to perform an operation.

So, the four of us set off. We entered a thick forest and started scrambling up steep ground. There was no path. The ladies walked in front of us in their bare feet. Each carried a stick with which they kept hitting the ground. When we asked them why they did that the answer was because of poisonous snakes! After an hour or so of strenuous walking we arrived at the church. It was in ruins and over-grown by trees and shrubs. There were no frescoes. A plaque informed us that they had been removed to a museum in Sofia.

So back down we went, the two barefooted ladies once again ahead of us beating the shrubs with sticks to chase away nasty snakes. Back in the town the ladies insisted on inviting us for lunch. They brought us to a little restaurant at the bank of a river.

As we could not understand the menu, we were led into the kitchen to look at the various dishes. We pointed at what we thought we would like to eat. We sat around a rickety wooden table. The owner appeared with a tablecloth. She spread it across the table with a grand gesture, as if it had been made of silk and gold, fit for a royal party. And, indeed, we were treated like royalty. I have never been back to Bulgaria, but the friendliness and hospitality of the people we met has secured a special place in my heart for that country.

3.5 A Journey into history

The history of Yugoslavia and her successor states is closely linked to the history of my own country, Austria. The historic connections are particularly poignant in my mother's birthplace, Sarajevo. When I was there for the first time in 1966, I stood on the same spot, (it was marked), as Gavrilo Princip who on 28th June 1914 assassinated the Archduke Franz Ferdinand, the successor to the throne of Austria-Hungary, and his wife, Countess Sophie Chotek. Nearby was a museum dedicated to this fatal event. I did not learn a lot from visiting it because the explanations were in Serbo-Croat, a language I learned later in life. Some 500 km to the West in Vienna is the marvellous *Heeresgeschichtliches Museum* (Military Museum). There the visitor can see the car in which the Austrian archduke and his wife were travelling when they were killed. Also, on display is the blood-drenched uniform the archduke was wearing. It is eerie to see these relics of an event that took place over a hundred years ago and triggered one of the greatest European catastrophes that changed the world forever.

Franz Ferdinand and Sophie Chotek were buried in the crypt of *Schloss Artstetten*, their private castle situated in the idyllic landscape north of the Danube in Lower Austria. Today the castle is the family home of the duchess Anita von Hohenberg and her husband. For reasons too complicated to explain here, the family of the assassinated archduke took the name Hohenberg. Anita von Hohenberg is a great granddaughter of Franz Ferdinand and of Sophie Chotek. On 17th May 2019 Ursula and I visited Schloss Artstetten with its excellent museum. When we arrived there a funeral was taking place. The crypt was closed to visitors but the museum was open. About a hundred and fifty guests were there, "all family" as one of the employees informed us. When the coffin was carried out of the chapel to be moved into the crypt a traditional brass band played a funeral march. We asked who had died and were told that we were witnessing the funeral of the Duke of Hohenberg. He had been in his late eighties and was a grandson of the assassinated archduke. After visiting the museum, we strolled around in the park. We observed the funeral party congregating in a fenced-off space behind the castle for drinks. Later we saw them move into the private rooms in the first floor for a meal.

Bosnia had been part of the Ottoman Empire for centuries before Austria-Hungary annexed it in 1908. About 250 km from Sarajevo my grandfather worked in the hospital of Bosanksi Novi (today Novi Grad). In 1910 he was made an honorary citizen of that town. After the collapse of the Habsburg Empire, he stayed in Yugoslavia and retired in Banja Luka, which now like Novi Grad is in the *Republica Srpska* of Bosnia-Herzegovina.

Sarajevo was hit very hard in the war that led to the breakup of Yugoslavia. Bosnia was a battleground between Catholic Croats, Orthodox Serbs and Muslims. This was not the first time Sarajevo became the victim of a war between Christians and Muslims. At the end of the 17th century the Austrian field marshal Prince Eugen of Savoy pushed the Turks out of Hungary and further east making sure that they would never again threaten Vienna. The Ottomans had unsuccessfully besieged the Imperial city twice, in 1529 and in 1683. After the battle of Zenta where he had routed the Turks, the Prince marched on Sarajevo. When the city refused to surrender on 23rd October 1697, he ordered his troops to ransack it for three days. Poor Sarajevo was burned down and completely destroyed.

In 1717 Eugen conquered the heavily fortified city of Belgrade. The fortress is called Kalemegdan and today is surrounded by a lovely park on an elevated spot from where one has great views over the river Sava. Whenever I visit my relations in Belgrade, we go for a stroll on Kalemegdan. There is a cemetery with the graves of Ottoman generals who defended the fortress and conquered far-away territories. The military commander of Belgrade in 1717 was Vezir Mükkerem Rumeli Valesi Bayeseli Taya-Sade Ibrahim Bassa. After peace was made between the Habsburgs and the Ottomans he served as ambassador in Vienna from 1719 to 1720. Prince Eugen of Savoy died in 1736. Three years later, in 1739, the Turks retook Belgrade.

Fifty more years went by till the Austrians once again besieged Belgrade and conquered it. The general commanding the Austrian forces was seventy-two year old Gideon Laudon, an experienced soldier and veteran of the Seven Years' War. The Habsburgs did not keep Belgrade very long. In the ensuing peace treaty, it was handed back to the Turks in 1791.

Laudon took Mükkerem Rumeli's marble sarcophagus to Vienna as a trophy. He also took with him two epitaphs and a beautiful Tughra, a calligraphic monogram of the sultan, all in marble. The epitaphs and the Tughra had been placed at Belgrade's Konstantinopel Gate after the Turks had retaken Kalemegdan and the city in 1739. The text of the epitaphs praises in grandiloquent language the victory Allah had granted the Ottomans over the infidel Austrians.

Gideon Laudon built himself a charming castle in Hadersdorf near Vienna. He died a year after his Belgrade military adventure and was buried in the Vienna Woods. Walking from Hadersdorf on the path leading further into the hills the hiker inevitably passes by Laudon's monumental grave. Not far from it, on the other side of the path, are the coffin of the Turkish commander of Belgrade, the two marble epitaphs and the Tughra.

In Sarajevo I stood on the spot from where Princip fired the fatal shots at the car in which Franz Ferdinand and Sophie were travelling. I saw that car and the blood-drenched uniform of the archduke in the Military Museum in Vienna and I accidentally witnessed the funeral of his grandson in Artstetten. I walked on Kale-megdan where Mükkerem Rumelis sarcophagus had stood before Laudon took it together with the epitaphs and the Tughra to Vienna and I look at these trophies in the Vienna Woods whenever I walk by them.

Travelling makes history come alive. It can open vistas into the past and make us aware of historic connections between places and persons and thus enrich our present.

Wounds of war in Mostar

Chapter 4: Ireland 1971 and 2001

4.1 Arrival in Ireland 1971

In 1969 I was at the University of Salzburg finishing my studies that I had begun in Vienna. At the end of a lecture the professor of Medieval German Literature announced that the University of Strathclyde in Glasgow was offering a post of German language assistant to an Austrian student. Anybody interested may contact him. I did not hesitate one second and went straight to see him. I knew nothing about Scotland except that it was quite far away. It was a spontaneous decision that changed my life.

The following two years, 1969 – 1971, I worked in Glasgow, Scotland, as a language assistant in German at the University of Strathclyde. Before I arrived there, I had heard a lot of negative stories about that city. It was said to have awful slums and the climate was hard to bear. The reality was not quite like this. Yes, there were poor areas but not more than in other big cities at the time. The climate was a bit cooler and it rained a lot, but when the sun was shining the surroundings of Glasgow showed themselves in all their glory. I loved the pubs and the Indian restaurants, which were very new to me, and I found the people to be quite friendly albeit a bit reserved.

When my two-year contract came to an end, I decided to stay a few years more in this part of Europe and sent applications to universities in Ireland. Galway replied favourably. When the university was about to send me the contract a post and telephone strike started in Britain. Throughout my time in Glasgow there had been a lot of industrial disputes. For a while we had power cuts because the employees of the electricity works were on strike. As the phone system was not yet fully automatic, one depended on operators to make a call to another city or country, and the operators were on strike. Luckily for me some of them broke the strike. If one kept ringing long enough there was a chance that one of the strikebreakers would pick up the phone. In this way I succeeded in getting in touch with the professor in Galway and confirm our agreement verbally. I was to start work in University College Galway in September 1971.

At that time the film *Ryan's Daughter* was showing in the cinemas. The wild beauty of the seascapes of county Kerry made a big impression on me and I imagined Ireland to be a country relatively untarnished by modern civilisation. I was very keen to visit Ireland before taking up my position so that I would get a feel for the place. The Easter break seemed to offer a good opportunity to travel there. My plan was to catch the night ferry from Stranraer in Scotland to Larne in Northern Ireland.

I was driving in the dark. The moon was shining and the road seemed empty. Suddenly, there was a cow standing in the middle of the road. I braked sharply, the car turned to the left and my right door hit the animal. The poor cow fell flat on its side and lay on the road for dead. While I was thinking of what to do, the animal suddenly got up, trotted into the field and disappeared. The car door was bashed in and I could not close it securely. I decided to drive back to Glasgow and have the damage repaired. Thus, ended my first attempt to get to Ireland.

My second attempt in June met with more success. As soon as I arrived in Galway, I went directly to the German Department. It took me some time to find it as it was situated outside the campus in a family house that had been taken over by the university. In this house were the German, French, Italian and Spanish departments. A cow was grazing in the front garden. How rural can a university be! I concluded that *Ryan's Daughter* had painted a true picture of Ireland. I passed by the grazing cow and entered the house. The two German language assistants welcomed me and phoned the Head of Department who very kindly invited me to dinner that evening.

I stayed in Galway four years. Ireland felt like a milder version of Scotland. By this I mean that the landscape around Galway reminded me of the Scottish Highlands, but the climate was softer and the mountains were easier to access. People were less reserved than in Scotland. Scottish towns of a size comparable to Galway were quiet in the evenings. Most people stayed in their houses in front of the TVs. Galway, however, sprang into life after sunset. The city at night had the flair of a southern European town that had been transposed to the north.

In the early seventies Galway was very different from what it is now. Tourists were few and the environment was largely untouched. I remember collecting wild mussels and bringing them home to cook. We could buy lobsters directly from the fishermen at ridiculously low prices. From the bridge near the Cathedral one could see wild salmon swimming up the River Corrib, and the first catch of the season was an event to be celebrated. Now the diseases spread by escaped farmed salmon are killing the wild salmon. A half-hour drive from Galway was Moran's of the Weir, a pub and restaurant that served native oysters and wild salmon with Guinness. Nowadays the West of Ireland is overrun with tourists. In the early seventies we had it all to ourselves.

Very soon after settling in Galway I joined the Galway Mountaineering Club. When I was a child, I had hiked a lot in the Austrian Alps with Uncle Erich. During my teenage years I had lost interest in alpinism and did not climb a mountain for years. In Galway I rediscovered my love of the mountains. Connemara and County Mayo offer everything a mountaineer can wish for. Although the summits are not higher than 700 m above sea level, they convey the feeling of being in alpine terrain. In contrast to the Alps, the mountains of Connemara, Mayo, Kerry and other parts of Ireland do not have marked trails. If one does not know how to use map and compass and to navigate in thick fog or in the dark, the Irish mountains (like those in Scotland) can be very dangerous. There are no huts either, and mobile phones very seldom get a signal. And if you rely on your GPS be aware that it is of no use when the battery runs out. If you want to get away from it all, the mountains of Connemara are the place for you!

4.2 The Skelligs 2001

When we children of the 20th and 21st century talk about getting away from it all, we mostly mean staying in a mountain hut or in a holiday cottage near the sea for a limited time. If we have to fetch our water from an outside well, we imagine that we are mastering the art of survival in extreme conditions. Yet, if our mobile phones get no reception, frustration sets in very quickly and we cannot wait to return to civilisation. The monks who settled on Skellig Michael off the coast of County Kerry in the sixth century A.D. were truly getting away from it all.

There are two Skellig islands. Little Skellig is a world-famous bird sanctuary and Skellig Michael, the bigger of the two islands, has a monastic settlement, which has been declared a UNESCO World Heritage Site. To get there by boat takes about an hour and a half. Because the sea is often rough one needs a good stomach to survive the boat trip without getting sick. When the swell is high, landing can be tricky. It can be difficult for the boat to dock, and passengers risk falling into the stormy sea when they jump from the boat to the pier. How the monks got there in their frail boats is hard to imagine. Getting there was the first stage of a process that selected the fittest. Once there, the monks never left. They stayed to the end of their lives surviving on what the sea provided and what they cultivated on their miserable plots. There was no water, except what could be collected from rainfall. Life expectancy must have been very short. Leaving the mainland behind, in order to lead a life of prayer on Skellig Michael, was like a suicide in slow motion. As the world was a vale of tears, it was best to escape from it as soon as possible and enter a better world in the hereafter.

I am afraid of visiting islands. My fear is that the weather changes and I get stuck there for days. Maybe the fact that Ireland is an island in the Atlantic Ocean, behind the bigger island of Britain, makes me permanently anxious to be cut off from my continental roots, and the thought of being unable to leave a small island off the coast of Ireland, even for a short time, makes me panic.

Another explanation may be that I suffer from mild claustrophobia. Being stuck on a small island is to me like being trapped in a lift.

In September 2001 we were holidaying in County Kerry. Our hotel was on the Ring of Kerry by the sea and close to the harbour, from where the boats leave for the Skelligs. The 11th September was a glorious day and for once I threw caution to the wind and allowed myself to be persuaded by Ursula to take the boat to Skellig Michael. I am very glad we went. I did not get seasick and the landing was unproblematic. We climbed the 670 steps to the top of the island. We saw the beehive stone dwellings where the monks lived and tried to imagine what it would be like to spend the rest of our lives on this remote island. The thought alone made me shudder. What a strong faith these monks must have had to endure such a life!

When we were returning to the mainland our skipper was highly agitated and told us that war had broken out. The United States was under attack from the Russians, skyscrapers were being bombed and all hell had broken loose. We did not believe him, but he insisted that he had heard it all on the radio. Back in the hotel we saw the videos of the planes flying into the twin towers and slowly it became clear to us what had happened. Thus, whenever I am asked where I was on *nine eleven*, I remember that it was the day we took the boat to the Skelligs.

The author on Benchoona Mountain
County Mayo

Chapter 5: USA 1993; an epic car journey

5.1 Why do we travel?

Why do some of us enjoy travelling? An obvious answer is that we like change. Being exposed to different kinds of people, customs, food, architecture, climate and landscapes can be uplifting and exhilarating. I always feel re-energised when I come back from a journey, no matter how long or short. It is said that one needs change. However, it is also true that many are afraid of change and crave the stability and security of the familiar. There are holiday-makers who do not seek the otherness when visiting a foreign country. All they want from the south of Spain is plenty of sun, an exciting nightlife and cheap booze. Apart from this they expect everything to be like at home. Instead of *mariscos* and *pulpos* they eat *fish and chips* or *Eisbein mit Sauerkraut,* they expect everyone to speak English or German, and they have no wish to explore the country they have chosen for their holidays. It is also possible that one and the same person sometimes desires change and at other times prefers to settle for the security of the familiar.

Other causes of wanderlust may lie deeper. When I was a student, I was obsessed with the idea of emigrating to the United States of America. In the late 1950s and early 1960s, the USA seemed to be a much better, more interesting and infinitely more exciting place to live and work than Austria and Europe. Although the war in Vietnam considerably diminished her attraction, the United States still appeared to be a desirable place for living and working. I never made it to the States, but ended up in Ireland instead. In hindsight, I am happy that I stayed in Europe. Would one really wish to live in a country with such an enormous gap between rich and poor, without a proper network of social security and where only those who can afford expensive health insurance receive good medical treatment? The idea I had then of living and working in America now appears to me as airy-fairy as were my dreams of becoming a sailor. Getting what one wishes for can be a bad thing and I was probably lucky not to get what I had wished for.

Be this as it may be, I visited the United States many times and enjoyed myself very much on every occasion. My first visit to the USA took place in the spring of 1991. The occasion was a conference on Austrian Literature in the University of California at Riverside. While I was there, I could not help imagining what it would have been like if I had moved to the United States. Travelling to foreign places can remind us that our lives could have been different. How would my life have been if I had emigrated from Austria to California? What would have happened to me if my parents had not left Belgrade for Vienna? What if I had been offered a post as a language assistant in Buenos Aires instead of in Glasgow? We are products of accidental circumstances. Travelling can make us aware of our unfulfilled potentials and of missed alternative lives.

5.2 An epic car journey

From 22nd to 25th April 1993 I attended the annual conference in the University of California at Riverside for the second time. These conferences, organised by the Head of the German Department, were wonderful events. I met many writers and interesting colleagues from different countries. Social life was great, the food was excellent and the weather was always fine, as one would expect in California.

This time I was on a half year sabbatical, which made it possible to spend a longer time in the USA. About two weeks before the start of the conference I was to give a lecture in Emory University in Atlanta and afterwards I was to lecture in Long Beach and Davis. So, here was the opportunity to take an epic trip across the United States and to get to know the country of my youthful dreams a bit better.

On 11th April, Ursula and I flew from Dublin to Atlanta and rented a car. We stayed in Atlanta for a few days and then drove across the continent to California, first to Riverside, then to Long

Beach and Los Angeles and, finally, to San Francisco and Davis. On 4th May we handed the car back at the airport in Los Angeles and returned to Dublin. Our journey may well qualify as a classic American road trip. It brought us through the states of Georgia, Alabama, Mississippi, Tennessee, Arkansas, Oklahoma, Texas, New Mexico and Arizona to California. En route to Riverside, we saw the Painted Desert and spent a few days in the Grand Canyon.

There is no better place for an epic car journey than the United States. Compared to Europe, the motorways were almost empty and most drivers religiously adhered to the speed limit even if it was set as low as fifty miles per hour, on roads devoid of traffic. Perhaps it is different today, but this was how it was then. All you had to do was to switch on the cruise control, lean back and let the car do the driving and avoid falling asleep. I began to understand why the motorcar was of such importance in the life of the average American.

Our plane landed in Atlanta at 5:00 p.m. local time. The air temperature was 27° C, a welcome change from cool and windy Dublin. We rented a small automatic Chevrolet Corsica and drove to the hotel that the German Department of Emory University had booked for us. The campus is situated in the suburb of Druid Hills, a beautiful park-like residential area famous for its blossoming trees, most of which were in full bloom when we were there. The creator was Frederick Law Olmsted, who is best known for designing Central Park in New York in partnership with Calvert Vaux. We were lucky to see Druid Hills at its best.

On the surface there was nothing in Atlanta that reminded the tourist of the racial tensions from which the Southern states had suffered so long. Martin Luther King was born there and assassinated in Memphis, Tennessee on 4th April 1968. He is buried in the Martin Luther King Jr. National Historical Park in Atlanta. In 1993 the city appeared to be peaceful and relaxed. We visited Stone Mountain, a huge monolith of granite, supposedly the biggest in the world. Around it a theme park has been created that leads the visitor through the history of the South. The reliefs of the generals of the Confederate Army, Robert E. Lee and Stonewall Jackson, and of Jefferson Davis, the president of the Confederate Stats, are carved into the granite monolith. A Mississippi steamer by name of Scarlet O'Hara cruises on an artificial lake. *Gone with the Wind* is Atlanta's *The Sound of Music*.

It became apparent that history was still very much part of the present when we got talking to a friendly couple sitting at the breakfast table next to us. They were there because the father of the husband was undergoing treatment for a heart disease in Emory University Hospital. When they learned that we came from Dublin and that I was to give a lecture in the German Department our conversation turned to educational matters. In their opinion most state schools and universities were lacking in discipline and failing to provide the students with a sound value system. Their children were studying in Bob Jones University in Granville, South Carolina, where they were sure to receive a solid conservative education that would shield them from drugs, alcohol, sexual promiscuity, homosexuality and all the other evils of modern society. Bob Jones had founded the university in the 1920s as an evangelical educational institution that promoted American conservative and Christian values and opposed liberalism, moral relativism, secularism, socialism and trade unions. Our table neighbours could not praise it enough and depicted it as an island of stability and security in a crumbling world.

When they proudly pointed out that Ian Paisley, the founder of the Free Presbyterian Church of Ulster and prominent Northern Irish politician, had received an honorary doctorate from Bob Jones University in 1966, our alarm bells began to ring. We knew Ian Paisley as the embodiment of religious fanaticism and sectarianism. He was viciously anti-Catholic, called the pope the Anti-Christ and incited violence against civil rights marchers in Northern Ireland. In the course of the conversation our table neighbours also revealed strong Anti-Yankee feelings. In their opinion the Southern States were a conquered territory and had been deprived of their identity. They commemorated the glorious performance of the Southern armies as if the civil war had happened only yesterday and they raised the confederate flag on every suitable occasion. We avoided talking about race, but from all they said we did not get the impression that they were champions of racial equality.

Well, there were two people who held deeply conservative, if not to say reactionary beliefs, who most likely were racist and who lived in a time bubble. They reminded me of the die-hard unionists in Northern Ireland who held strong sectarian views and behaved as if they were still living in the time of the Reformation. But like so many of the extreme Unionists these reactionary Confederates were friendly, well-mannered and good company. This might well have changed if we had allowed the conversation to take a serious turn. But we were guests in Atlanta and had no intention of rocking the boat.

On our first day in Atlanta, we wanted to see the German department and meet some of the colleagues with whom I had corresponded. We had no success. Nobody seemed to know where it was. At one stage we ended up in a centre of biological research. Apparently, the person who had given us directions thought that "German" had something to do with germs. In the evening we met the Head of the German department and his wife, in a charming restaurant with a garden. This is a rare thing in the United States where the tradition of eating outdoors does not seem to exist (except, of course, in private gardens). In Vienna restaurants with a back garden are not uncommon. If there is no back garden, very often tables and chairs are placed on the pavement. These improvised pavement "gardens" are called *Schanigarten*. In the summer Vienna turns into one big *Schanigarten*. Americans seem to prefer to dine in air-conditioned rooms. This is a pity because in so many parts of the States the conditions are perfect for outdoor dining. The restaurant we were brought to was thus unusual. I chose a trout for main course. It was stuffed with spinach and topped with cheese so that the taste of the fish was almost totally concealed. The waiter informed me proudly that the trout was farmed.

Next day the Head of Department collected us from the hotel and drove us to the German Department where I delivered my lecture and met the students and colleagues. Everybody was extremely friendly and seemingly pleased to meet a guest from Europe. Like in so many German Departments in the USA and in South America the staff consisted mostly of German and Austrian expats. They had done what I had dreamed of doing in the late sixties and early seventies: they had left their homeland because they felt that life in the New World would be more rewarding than in old Europe. They had adapted to the American way of life; some had married American citizens and life in general was good. Nevertheless, I got the impression that many of them were homesick. Most still had family members in Europe, some had bought a house or an apartment in their country of origin and were spending as much time there as their work allowed and others hoped to return "home" after retirement.

A few weeks later I met a colleague in Davis who could not wait to retire and go back to Europe. He was the most atypical Northern Irish Protestant I have ever met. Nationalists who desire a united Ireland are normally Catholics while most Protestants are Unionists. They consider themselves British and wish to maintain the union between Northern Ireland and Britain. This colleague, however, was a Protestant *and* an Irish Nationalist! He was in his mid-fifties and talked at every opportunity about his plan to buy a property in the Republic of Ireland and retire there as soon as he had reached retirement age. I do not know if he ever realised his dream. In 1993 property in Ireland was still affordable. A few years later house prices spiralled out of control and he may have had no option but to stay where he was.

After leaving Atlanta we spent a week on the road driving to California. On the first day we got as far as Brinkley in Arkansas having passed by Birmingham, Alabama and Memphis, Tennessee. Somewhere we stopped for lunch in a Pizza Hut. The waitress who told us that she was of Irish descent was very friendly and overweight. When she guided us to the buffet she said: "You can eat as much as you can hold".

We spent that night near Brinkley in a Super 8 Motel. The bed sheets looked like they had not been changed. When we complained, somebody came and changed them quite nonchalantly and without offering an apology. Sitting down for dinner we ordered blackened fish, that is to say a fresh water fish grilled on charcoal and burned black on the outside. This is a speciality of that area worth trying. When I asked what kind of wine they had, the waitress said: "Sorry, we do not have wine." This was a bit strange, but we decided that beer might do in an emergency. I ordered two beers but was told: "Sorry, we do not have beer." "What kind of drinks do you have?" I asked somewhat bewildered. "We have Coca Cola, lemonade, mineral water...." It turned out that we were in a "dry county". I had never heard of this before but believe that it is quite common in the Bible Belt of the United States. It signifies an area with a radius of about twenty or thirty miles within which no alcoholic drinks are available. We had no choice but to drink water with our fish.

The next leg of our road trip brought us through Fort Smyth, Fayetteville and Rogers to Prairie Creek. There we visited friends who had retired and bought a house in a forest near Beaver Lake. Tom and Shirley owned a motorboat and took us for a cruise on the lake in the afternoon. Beaver Lake was created by damming up White River and is full of side arms stretching out in all directions, which makes for challenging navigation.

Our friends' house was spacious and comfortable, the kitchen was ultramodern, a chef's dream. However, instead of preparing a meal for us in this splendid kitchen our hosts decided to take us to a restaurant. When I was a teenager the term "American kitchen" stood for the ultimate in kitchen design. On various journeys through the United States and Canada we saw quite a few of these wonderful kitchens with fridges, cookers, and ovens twice the size of those in Europe, but we never had the pleasure of eating a meal prepared in one of them. North Americans do not seem to like to cook for their guests. The restaurant our friends had chosen was excellent. The speciality was fish from either fresh or salt water. Once again, however, we were in one of those dreaded "dry counties". Luckily, this time it did not matter because Tom was a member of a club that entitled him to order alcoholic drinks to go with the meal. So, we could accompany our delicious seafood with good wine.

Our journey to Riverside continued for another six days. The drive through Oklahoma, Texas and New Mexico was monotonous and seemingly endless. In the middle of nowhere we had lunch in a supposedly native Indian restaurant. The food was disappointing, and most of the customers looked rather downtrodden. All kept their caps on while eating. I have repeatedly noticed the sad look of Native Americans in the United States. Their counterparts in Ecuador appear to be happier. Although their ancestors also were abused and suppressed by the conquistadors and still suffer considerable discrimination today, their lot appears to be somewhat better than that of their brothers and sisters in North America. This is certainly true in those parts of Ecuador, where indigenous people make up the majority. An example is Otavalo, a city some 100 km north of the capital Quito, whose weekly indigenous market is a most joyful experience that has no counterpart anywhere in the United States. Later in the afternoon we stopped near Amarillo for a coffee break. Everybody in the café was black. Although we must have looked very conspicuous with our white skins, we encountered no hostility. While we drank our coffee, we listened to the conversation of a group of men at the table next to us. They spoke with a wonderful southern drawl of which we did not understand one word. It sounded like music.

After overnighting in Tucumcari, we continued driving through New Mexico and then on to Arizona. The weather was unusually dull, but it improved towards the evening, enough to enable us to appreciate the colours of the Painted Desert where we spent two hours (far too little, I know, but we were pressed for time). That day the drive seemed endless. The emptiness and the loneliness of the landscape were overwhelming. Roads without traffic, leading through a desert-like landscape without any sign of human habitation for miles, that seem to stretch to infinity, not only exist in American movies and TV series like *Breaking Bad*, but also in reality!

While driving we listened to the radio and soon became addicted to Rush Limbaugh. First we found his undisguised contempt for and hatred of liberal views, homosexuals and ethnic minorities disturbing. How could that be tolerated? Did freedom of speech mean that incitement of hatred had to be allowed? At the same time we could not help admiring his command of the English language and his superb rhetoric. After a while we began to find his tirades sort of entertaining. He certainly kept us awake.

We came to a town called Holbrook. As this had been the maiden name of Ursula's grandmother we decided to stay there for the night. If one were to look for a place that illustrated perfectly the phrase *in the middle of nowhere* one need to go no further. Located in Navajo County with a population of about 5,000 Holbrook looked like a town out of a Wild West movie. And, indeed, it was a typical Wild West town. In 1881 it was connected to the railway line and was named after Henry Randolph Holbrook who was the chief engineer of the *Atlantic and Pacific Railroad.* In 1887 one of the most famous shootouts of the Wild West took place there. On 4th September of that year Sheriff Perry Owens came to Holbrook to arrest Andy Blevins for horse theft. When Andy Blevins, his two brothers and a friend resisted arrest and opened fire, the Sheriff singlehandedly shot dead all but one of the brothers.

We drove into Holbrook at about 6:00 p.m. and booked into a Budget Inn located in the restaurant and hotel strip of the town. As usual after a long drive we were hungry and looked forward to a good meal. Wherever we turned we saw nothing but the likes of Denny, Sizzler and McDonald. We asked the man at the reception if he knew of a place where we could get real food and he recommended a restaurant in a side street that turned out to be a very pleasant surprise. The couple that ran the place knew how to prepare a good steak. We enjoyed the food and emptied a bottle of Californian red wine. Thus, the day came to pleasant end.

The highlight of our epic road trip was a two night stay (19th and 20th April) in Moqui Lodge near the Grand Canyon National Park. En route there we passed the Grand Canyon Airport, where we saw a sign advertising flights over the canyons. Spontaneously we decided to enquire about flights and were happy to hear that a light plane would take off in half an hour. Thus, we first saw the canyons from the air. We were six passengers: four Israelis and the two of us. The pilot had a hand-drawn map in front of him that highlighted the turning points of the route. I was a little astonished that he did not have a more high tech route finder than this. However, low tech as his little sheet of paper may have been, it did the job.

We arrived in Moqui lodge in the afternoon and had enough time to drive alongside the Eastern Rim and to take photographs of the breath-taking sunsets between 6:00 and 6:30 p.m. In the morning of the following day, we walked towards the bottom of the valley. When hiking in the mountains one normally walks uphill first and then downhill. Hiking in the Canyon is the reverse: first comes the descent and then the ascent. To get to the valley floor, one has to descend 1000 m. This is inevitably followed by an ascent of 1,000 m on the same day unless one has booked accommodation in the valley. We descended for about two hours and got beyond Cedar Crest. As there were plenty of warnings about the dangers of dehydration and heat strokes, we decided to go back before the midday heat. Later we regretted this decision. We were about one hour from the bottom. It was April and the temperatures were no higher than what we were used to from the Austrian Alps in summer. The severe warnings were directed at tourists who had no experience of hiking in the mountains. In hindsight we realised that we would have had no problems going down and up in one day.

We finished the day by driving alongside the Western rim watching and photographing more glorious sunsets. It was magical. Not only were the sunsets beautiful beyond words, so was the whole atmosphere that descended upon the place. There were few tourists. When the sun began to set and the red colours of the canyons began to glow, not a sound could be heard. It felt as if we were in a huge open-air church and under the spell of a tremendous mystery.

Chapter 6: The German Democratic Republic 1994

6.1 The Iron Curtain

Travelling into Communist countries before glasnost and the fall of the Berlin Wall was no big deal for me as an Austrian. I had been to Yugoslavia the first time while I was still in high school. I went there again with my American friend Ann, with whom I also visited Czechoslovakia in 1966 and Bulgaria in 1967. I have fond memories of Yugoslavia and of Bulgaria. Czechoslovakia was different. Ann and I went there two years before the short-lived Prague Spring. While we were checking into the hotel some bystanders made unpleasant remarks about Germans. This happened again and again. People thought that we were German and made us feel unwelcome. We had travelled to Prague in Ann's car. One day she drove into a petrol station and approached the pump in the wrong way. The attendant rushed to the car and shouted in German: *In Deutschland fährt man wohl nicht rechts!* (Apparently, in Germany you do not drive on the right side). Ann was quite taken aback and when she replied in English that she was not German but American he immediately changed his behaviour. Suddenly he was all apologies and overly friendly. The speed with which he changed was utterly amazing. When we drove back into Austria, the Czech border police took half an hour to search our suitcases and bags. They even used mirrors to look under the car! The whole journey had been an unpleasant experience, and I did not visit that country again until long after the Communist regime had ended.

An even more unpleasant country to visit was the DDR, the *Deutsche Demokratische Republik* (German Democratic Republic). There was never any problem in travelling around Yugoslavia. Once in the country one could move around freely and stay wherever one wished. Yugoslavs could travel to the West comparatively easily. Bulgaria eased the visa restrictions in 1967 and Western tourists were free to go where they liked. Even in Czechoslovakia tourists could go anywhere. However, if Western tourists wanted to visit the DDR, they had to inform the authorities exactly where they were going. They had to produce a daily plan of their route. You could be sure that the police checked that any given time you were where you were supposed to be.

In 1971 I visited a friend in West Berlin. In order to get from Germany to West Berlin by car or by train one had to go through the DDR. Leaving the train or the motorway was strictly forbidden. There were warning signs at the exit points of the motorway reminding the traveller that only citizens of the DDR were allowed to drive off. The territory between West Germany and West Berlin was commonly referred to as *die Zone*. Entering and leaving *die Zone* one had to cross heavily fortified checkpoints. There were watchtowers with armed soldiers who would shoot anybody who attempted to escape from the Communist paradise.

Visiting my friend in West Berlin in 1971 was the only time I had to enter (albeit only on transit) the territory of what was the German Democratic Republic from the end or World War II to the collapse of the Soviet Union and the fall of the Berlin Wall. My dislike of the DDR prevented me from travelling there and supporting its economy. Some of my leftist friends did not agree with me and pointed to the many good things communism had to offer such as free healthcare, free education and affordable accommodation for everybody. All of these achievements were in my opinion invalidated by the fact that the whole country was a prison. Nobody was allowed to leave without permission. *Republikflucht* (escape from the Republic) was a crime that was severely punished, and persons who were caught crossing the border illegally were often shot dead. Justifying this deadly policy by pointing to the "positive" sides of the DDR regime seemed to me like justifying Hitler's gas chambers by referring to the recovery of the economy and the creation of near full employment achieved by the Nazis. I had to wait until the communist nightmare finally ended to see Leipzig, Dresden, Meissen and the places where Goethe, Schiller and Martin Luther had lived.

6.2 Dresden and Leipzig

After the Berlin Wall fell in 1990 and Germany was unified, we met two couples from the former German Democratic Republic. Gerhard and Inge were from Dresden and we got to know them when they visited Ireland. A few weeks later a professor of Drama in Leipzig and his wife attended a conference in Dublin that I had organised. They all stayed as guests in our house. In March 1994 we decided to drive to Thuringia and Saxony and visit both couples. Knowing somebody in a strange place is always a great asset. After overnighting with friends in Hagen near Bonn we drove to Eisenach in Thuringia on 14th March.

Eisenach is the town where Johann Sebastian Bach was born in 1685. Martin Luther translated the Bible, while he was staying in the Wartburg Castle above the town from May 1521 to March 1522. There are other events associated with Eisenach to which I will refer later. From my schooldays on I had always wanted to see the castle where Martin Luther went into hiding after he had refused to recant his heretical views at the Diet of Worms. The Elector of Saxony, Frederick the Wise, gave him sanctuary in the Wartburg. Luther stayed there under the name of Junker Jörg and translated the Bible from Greek into German.

Scholarly works are generally considered to be of importance only within the boundaries of the academic ivory tower. Luther transcended this boundary. His translation of the Bible into a popular idiom that could be understood by most speakers of the many different German dialects laid the foundation for a common German language. Without Luther's Bible the north and the south of Germany would very likely speak different languages today. Frederick almost certainly saved Luther from suffering the fate of his predecessor Jan Hus who was burnt at the stake for his views a hundred years earlier. His work in many ways anticipated those of the German reformer. Luther's survival secured the success of the Reformation that changed Germany and Europe.

Our first visit was to the Wartburg to see the room where Luther had lived and worked. Because the castle fell into disarray during the Thirty Years War the original furniture has been lost and the room was refurbished around 1900. But it still is the room where it all had happened. A writing desk, a pen, ink and paper were all Martin Luther needed. His achievement was comparable to discoverers like Columbus and Magellan who sailed into the unknown, in tiny wooden ships that depended entirely on the elements.

The other two events for which the Wartburg is remembered are the *Sängerkrieg*, a contest of German *Minnesingers* (troubadours) that allegedly took place at the beginning of the 13th century, and the *Wartburgfest* of 18th October 1817. While the first is pure fiction the second is part of German history. Five hundred students gathered there to demand the formation of a unified national state, a German constitution and freedom of speech. The Wartburg was chosen because it was there that Luther had laid the foundation of a common German language. Luther was considered by these students to have been a champion of German nationhood. Three hundred years earlier, on 31st October 1517, he had nailed his 95 theses to the door of the church of Wittenberg and started the movement against the papacy in Rome. Although the students who attended the *Wartburgfest* saw themselves as defenders of liberty and tolerance, they burnt in effigy the Code Napoléon and books that they considered to promote reactionary ideas. The contemporary German poet Heinrich Heine was horrified by this action and accused the students of committing "Dummheiten, die des blödsinnigsten Mittelalters würdig waren" (stupidities worthy of the most idiotic Middle Ages) and of practicing a "beschränkte(n) Teutomanismus, der viel von Liebe und Glaube greint, dessen Liebe aber nichts anderes war als der Haß des Fremden" (a narrow minded manic teutonism that talked much of love and faith yet was nothing but hatred of everything foreign).

Heine's words showed an uncanny political foresight. Today's successors of the historic *Burschenschaften* (student fraternities) in Germany and Austria are hotbeds of right-wing ideas. Most of the members of Austria's far right FPÖ (*Freiheitliche Partei Österreichs / Austrian Freedom Party*) are also members of such *teutomanische Burschenschaften*! Their policy is still characterized by a narrow-minded idealization of everything *Teutonic* and by xenophobia, as Heinrich Heine had described it two hundred years ago.

After having seen Luther's room, we looked at the impressive fresco representing the legendary *Sängerkrieg* created by Moritz von Schwind in 1854. We then continued our journey to Dresden. Gerhard and Inge had invited us to stay with them in their apartment. They welcomed us with an excellent dinner. Both were retired. Gerhard had worked as an engineer for the state-owned railways. Their experience of the changeover from communism to Western democracy after the unification of Germany was not all positive. True, they now could travel freely wherever they wanted, and they were financially somewhat better off, but the onslaught of unbridled capitalism made them feel worried and anxious. As they saw it, the socialist system had guaranteed a simple but secure life for everybody and had prevented the income gap between low and high earners becoming as wide as it was in the West. Now socialism was being replaced by brutal competition and a culture of greed. Gerhard and Inge felt that *unification* was a euphemism for *takeover* or *colonisation*. Although they were far from defending the wrongs of the East German communist regime, they were socialists at heart and had hoped that the DDR after the fall of the Berlin Wall would go *einen dritten Weg* (a third way) between that of Western capitalism and Soviet style communism. It was a hope that they shared with many intellectuals in both East and West, and which was not fulfilled. Driving into Dresden the signs of change could be clearly seen. The city was a building site full of huge cranes. All the building contracts were given to Western firms. There was nothing in it for indigenous industries. It was becoming clear who were the winners and who were the losers in the new era.

Gerhard and Inge were fond of classical music and they knew that we shared their enthusiasm. They surprised us with opera tickets for the next day. We were to attend a performance of *Capriccio* by Richard Strauss in the famous Dresden Opera House. Built by Gottfried Semper between 1838 and 1841 it is justly considered to be one of the most beautiful opera houses in the world. After it burnt down in 1869, Semper was given the task of rebuilding it. The new house opened in 1878. Many operas had their world premiers in either the old or the new house. The impressive list includes Richard Wagner's *Rienzi* (1842), *The Flying Dutchman* (1843) and *Tannhäuser* (1845) and Richard Strauss' *Der Rosenkavalier* (1911). During the terrible bombing of Dresden in 1945, by the British and Americans, it was once again destroyed in the ensuing firestorm. It was lovingly restored to its 1878 appearance under the communist regime, and the house reopened on 13th March 1985 with Carl Maria von Weber's *Der Freischütz*. The technical facilities were brought up to 20th century standards. According to our hosts it was rumoured that the air conditioning system was equipped with sophisticated bugging devices so that the STASI (the state security department) could overhear the conversation of everybody in the audience. If these devices really existed, they had been removed after unification. At least so everybody assumed.

Two days later we arrived in Leipzig and visited the professor and his wife. They could not put us up in their apartment, but they gave us coffee and cake. We were served refreshments on inherited Meissen porcelain. After this the professor took us on a tour of the city. He brought us to the two main churches, the *Thomaskirche*, St Thomas Church and the *Nikolaikirche*, St Nikolas Church.

The St Thomas Church is first and foremost known as the place where Johann Sebastian Bach worked as director of music and where he is buried. Luther preached there in 1539. The St Nikolas Church became well known during the demonstrations for more personal freedom that took place in 1989, one year before the fall of the Berlin Wall. The demonstrators congregated around pastor Christian Führer, who every Monday held prayers in his church protesting against the arms race between East and West. Soon these meetings became full-fledged protest marches against the regime.

For a while the Lutheran church was central to the struggle for change. We happened to enter the church while a service was going on. Our host told us that the preacher was the very Pastor Christian Führer who had played such a pivotal role during *die Wende* (turning point), that ultimately led to the unification of Germany. Now the church was almost empty. Where were all those enthusiastic people who had turned to the church for support in the critical year before the fall of the Berlin Wall and whose demands were courageously backed by the Lutheran pastor? *Der dritte Weg* envisaged by the protesters of 1989 proved to be a chimera. Gerhard and Inge had good reason to be disillusioned.

From 16th to 19th October 1813 the surroundings of Leipzig were the scene of a decisive battle between Napoleon's Grande Armée and the allied Austrians, Russians, Prussians and Swedes. The allies, under the supreme command of the Austrian field marshal Karl Phillip zu Schwarzenberg, defeated Napoleon who afterwards was banished to the island of Elba. The death toll was enormous. Our host took us to the monument that was erected a hundred years later. It lists the numbers of the dead and wounded on both sides. It makes horrific reading; 38,000 French, 22,000 Russians, 16,600 Prussians, 14,400 Austrians, 200 Swedes. The number of casualties totalled 91,200! This was 26,200 more than the dead and wounded at Waterloo two years later.

The *Völkerschlacht bei Leipzig* (the battle of the peoples near Leipzig) was the biggest battle fought in the entire 19th century. Europe was a battlefield not only in the 19th and 20th centuries. Throughout history European dynasties and nations had constantly fought each other. Peace was the exception. One of the original aims of the European Union was to prevent further wars on our continent. At its heart the European Union is a peace project. I will never understand why the British who voted for Brexit did not appreciate this or did not care.

To crown the day, our host took us for dinner to the city's best-known restaurant. *Auerbachs Keller* dates back to the 16th century and has been immortalized by Goethe, who set one of the scenes of his play *Faust* there. After our pleasant meal it was time to look for a place to stay for the night. All the hotels in Dresden were big luxury hotels that had been frequented by the bosses of the Communist Party and their pals. Simple *Pensionen* or B&B within our price range did not exist. The professor thought that we would find a guesthouse en route to Meissen. So, off we drove into the night. It was 9:00 p.m. and snowing. We passed a few roadside inns, but they were closed. Near Meissen we saw a brand-new hotel that looked as if it had been completed only yesterday. As it was now 10:00 p.m. we decided to stay there. We drove to the main entrance and before we could get out of the car two liveried footmen in 18th century attire, with white powdered wigs, rushed towards us and insisted on carrying our luggage. We had to pay an exorbitant price for this privilege.

Chapter 7: Ecuador 1995 – 2001

7.1 Quito 1995

14th July 1995, 5:00 p.m. local time. Ursula and I were on the flight to Ecuador with twenty friends from our Irish hiking clubs, the *Ramblers* and *Wayfarers*. Our *Iberia* plane was flying over Columbia. On the screens in front of our seats we could see exactly where we were. Beneath us was Medellin. Thick clouds blocked the view. We all knew the name of Medellin from reports about the Columbian drug cartels and from American action movies such as *Clear and Present Danger*, where Harrison Ford survived all kinds of horrendous adventures in the war between the drug barons and the Drug Enforcement Agency (DEA) of the United States. One year later I read *Noticia de un secuestro* by Gabriel García Márquez, a documentary report that was even more exciting than the fantasies of Hollywood. It told how the Columbian police finally hunted down the drug boss Pablo Escobar after he had abducted a number of journalists and TV personalities. We were still 30,000 feet above sea level and the thermometer showed a temperature of minus 40° C. In an hour we would be landing in Quito. I knew that the Andes were beneath us and was disappointed not to see them. We were descending very slowly. Twenty minutes before landing we were still flying at an altitude of 24,000 feet.

We were now above Otavalo, a small town some eighty kilometres north of Quito about which I had read in my travel books. High mountains surround it and it is a centre of indigenous culture noted for its Saturday markets. A few minutes later we were very near Quito and there was still no sign of losing height. Then, suddenly we dropped to 15,000 feet in what seemed to me to be a few seconds. The clouds were breaking up and we saw the mountains. On my left a gigantic cone covered in snow and ice was sticking its peak into the now blue sky. Somebody said that this was *El Cotopaxi*. It is almost 6,000 m high and believed to be the highest active volcano in the world. I looked at it in awe and got a bit worried about our ambition to climb it. We obviously had overshot Quito and were now approaching the city from a southerly direction. The plane had dropped to under 12,000 feet and was descending fast. On both sides mountains appeared whose peaks were now above us. When we turned right, we saw blue sky on our left and green slopes on our right whose steepness was accentuated by the bank angle of the aeroplane. When we turned left, the situation reversed. Approaching the Ecuadorian capital, we seemed to be meandering between mountains.

Suddenly we got a view of Quito, a sea of stone that spilled over into the foothills of the mountains. On the left appeared the two local volcanoes, *Guagua Pichincha* and *Rucu Pichincha*. The aeroplane was still on a slalom course and I had given up trying to follow the numerous turns. All of a sudden, green fields appeared underneath us, then the runway. Left and right of the runway were houses. The airport seemed to be situated in the middle of a built-up area. This impression turned out to be correct; a few days later I read a report in a local newspaper about the dangers of Quito International Airport. It was not unusual that planes overshot the runway and ended up in someone's front garden or sitting room. Our plane now touched the runway and jumped back into the air before staying on the runway and braking sharply. We stopped well before we hit any of the houses. The passengers spontaneously applauded. We were in Quito, capital of Ecuador. It was my first time in South America.

At 6:30 p.m. we stepped out of the aeroplane. As we were walking across the tarmacadam to the arrival hall, we could see big mountains surrounding us on all sides. It became obvious why our pilot had to approach the airfield like a slalom skier and why jumbo jets never landed in Quito. (I believe that in the meantime a new and safer airport has been built). The sky was now clear and it was fast getting dark but the snow-covered peaks still shimmered golden in the setting sun. Somebody pointed out *El Cayambe* in the North East. With its 5,700 m this is Ecuador's third highest mountain and straddles the equator. There is no higher point on the equator anywhere on earth than the summit of Cayambe.

The airport was small. Only a few planes were parked there. The arrival hall was also small and the architecture can be best described as modest. The formalities of immigration were dealt with promptly and politely. After having picked up our luggage and changed money we stepped out of the airport. It was now 7:00 p.m. and pitch dark. Just as I started looking for taxis for the twenty-two people in our group a small man of plump build approached me and asked if I happened to be *el señor Herzmann*. He introduced himself as the owner of the *Hotel Viena Internacional* into which we were booked. He had arrived with a bus to bring us to his hotel. I had not expected this and was grateful and impressed.

The bus looked like the buses I remembered from the 1950s. There were no pneumatic doors and the hood with the engine protruded a few metres forward of the front. Inside was the smell of petrol that used to make me sick when I was a child. What distinguished this bus from the buses of my childhood were the colour and the decorations. Austrian buses belonged to the state-run postal services. They were painted yellow and were not embellished by any kind of knickknacks. This bus displayed an array of bright colours and the area around the driver's seat was covered with holy pictures, rosaries, figurines and plenty of wise sayings such as *Mi mujer está casada. Yo soy soltero*; My wife is married; I am a bachelor.

The bus rattled through the dimly lit streets. Traffic was dense and chaotic. The buildings looked rather shabby. Many side streets were completely unlit. The closer we came to the city centre, where our hotel was situated, the more crowded the streets became. We saw indigenous people sitting on the pavement, offering their wares for sale. There were food stalls and in some corners there were open fires, where people were cooking or simply warming themselves. Everything seemed to be happening in the streets. One could easily pick out the indigenous population by their beautiful straight black hair. Most wore their native costumes, felt hats, scarfs and ponchos. The women had their necks and arms decorated with golden necklaces and bracelets. They carried small children on their backs, wrapped in a cloth. Our hotel was right in the middle of all this commotion. The bus stopped outside and when unloading our luggage we caused a traffic-jam.

The *Hotel Viena Internacional* must once have been a town house of a rich Quiteño. It was built towards the end of the 19th century in the Spanish Colonial style, with a big patio and the living quarters around it on four sides. There was no roof over the patio. We could see the sky and when we walked up to the second level we got a glimpse of a few church towers that were a good bit higher than the hotel and therefore well visible. Exotic flowers and shrubs surrounded the fountain on the patio. In the entrance hall beside the reception stood a larger-than-life size statue of Christ Crucified. When Ursula and I walked up to our room on the second floor we came across The Risen Christ on the half landing. He, too, was larger than life.

On this our first evening most of our group hardly dared to venture outside the hotel. We had read that the inner city was not a safe place to walk around. Some of us, however, could not resist our curiosity and we walked around the side streets, looking at the stalls, and the throngs of people wheeling and dealing in everything imaginable. Dr Tom, one of the most intrepid travellers of our group, bought a grilled chicken and some maize dish from one of the many stalls. We expected him to be sick the next day but he suffered no ill effects. During our stay Dr Tom tried in vain to get food poisoning by insisting on eating in the most suspect dives, but his good health never suffered.

Immediately outside the hotel entrance was a huge hole. Obviously urgent repairs were being carried out on the underground piping system. Whoever was responsible for that job had not bothered protecting the hole or putting up any warning signs. It would have been the easiest thing in the world to step out of the hotel, fall into this hole and disappear into the subterranean regions of the

Ecuadorian capital. We soon realised that the hole in front of our hotel was not the only one. It was highly advisable to keep at least one eye on the ground at all times. We also saw some impressive entrances to subterranean caves in the middle of the streets. Car drivers seemed to be well used to skilfully avoiding them.

Two years later I returned with a group of hikers, with the intention of spending more time in the Andes. When I went to buy provisions for a hike I fell into a hole outside the shop. I do not remember falling, I heard a crash and suddenly found myself up to my waist in this hole, one leg on the bottom the other one on the pavement. The shopkeeper ran out of the shop and helped me out. She brought me inside sat me down on a chair and gave me a glass of water. I was quite shaken and my left ankle was badly bruised. The shopkeeper told me that the corporation simply did not give a damn about the state of the streets. A few days ago a tourist from Argentina had fallen into the very same hole.

Later in the day we saw a group of blind people staging a protest against the lack of facilities for blind pedestrians. Nobody took any notice.

In spite of the *huecos* that pose such a grave danger to unsuspecting pedestrians Quito is a city well worth visiting. Our hotel was in the historic centre, which was declared a UNESCO World Heritage Site in 1978. According to Wikipedia the Ecuadorian capital has "the largest, least-altered, and best-preserved historic centre in the Americas". It was a five-minute walk to the main square flanked by the marvellous Church of San Francisco. Near the square we discovered a restaurant that had a very smart cocktail bar and served excellent food in elegant surroundings. *La Cueva del Oso* (The Bear's Cave) became our regular.

7.2 Rucu Pichincha 1995; an adventure in the Andes

El Cotopaxi, at 5,890 m, is considered the world's highest active volcano. The highest mountain of Ecuador, *El Chimborazo* at 6,300 m, was long thought to be the highest in the world. Because the globe is shaped like a rugby ball, the summit of Chimborazo is the point furthest away from the centre of the earth. The peak of Cayambe is 5,700 m above sea level and thus the highest point anywhere on the equator. There are many other mountains of over 5,000 m. They lie to the east and west of the Pan-American Highway, *La Panamericana* that starts in Alaska and leads through Canada, the United States, Mexico, Central and South America, all the way down to Patagonia. Apart from Cayambe, Cotopaxi and Chimborazo there are many more mountains, most of them volcanoes, with exotic sounding names: *Cotacachi, Rucu Pichincha* and *Guaga Pichincha, Carihuairazo, Tungurahua* and *Sangay*. Sangay is permanently active and very dangerous to climb. Cotoacachi, Chimborazo and Cayambe are said to be extinct. However, climbing Cayambe one can smell sulphur, which indicates that there is still some activity. Rucu Pichincha, near Quito, has long been extinct but neighbouring Guagua Pichincha erupted violently in 1999, covering the whole city in ash for weeks. Shortly after Guagua Pichincha calmed down, Tungurahua at the rim of the Amazonian basin began to spit lava and fire and threatened the little town of Baños, which had to be evacuated for three months.

When the German scientist and explorer Alexander von Humboldt travelled to Ecuador, at the beginning of the 18th century, he called the central valley dividing the Eastern and the Western Cordilleras of Ecuador very appropriately the "Avenue of the Volcanoes".

All these mountains are well worth climbing. They are easily accessible. It is possible to drive to the start of most of the climbs. Cotopaxi and Chimborazo have a hut at an altitude of about 5,000 m. From there one can reach the summit in one big push. This normally requires leaving the hut by midnight and returning to it by midday. In this way one avoids walking on the glacier after the snow has become too soft. Of course, it is necessary to be acclimatised and fit to do this. In Ecuador it is possible to climb quite a few really big mountains in a few weeks.

Cotopaxi is the most climbed mountain in Ecuador. It has a perfect cone shape, the weather tends to be better than on other high peaks in the country and the hut is one of the best equipped. The regular route to the summit of Cotopaxi starts from the Refugio José Ribas situated at 4,800 m on the north side of the mountain. Starting from Quito one can reach the car park 200 m below the hut in a few hours. From the car park it is an hour's walk to the refuge from where it is possible to summit and return in one long day. Some guidebooks describe the route as non-technical. By this is meant that no proper ice climbing techniques are required. However, one must know how to handle rope, ice axe and crampons and have experience in crossing crevasses. Those who lack these skills should take a good guide. The same applies to the regular route to the summit of Chimborazo.

On our first visit in the summer of 1995 our plan was not to hike or to climb but to explore the country's cultural and natural sites, the colonial towns, the Inca ruins, the rainforest, the coast and the Galapagos Islands. After everything was arranged somebody in the group suggested that we should have a go at Cotopaxi. Because Ursula and I tried to keep everybody happy and, I must admit, because I was tempted to have a go myself, we added Cotopaxi to our itinerary. I began to search the guidebooks for mountain guides, and, after receiving various offers I decided on Freddy Ramirez from *Sierra Nevada Expeditions* in Quito. He turned out to be an excellent guide with whom I soon became friends and whom I employed many more times on later trips to the Andes. The problem was that the only slot he could offer for climbing Cotopaxi fell into the first week of our journey when we would not be sufficiently acclimatised. Nevertheless, five of us decided to make the attempt. They were Pat L, Doreen, Dr Tom, Ted and myself. It was, of course, pure madness.

We arrived in Quito on the evening of Friday, 14th July. On Monday we were supposed to head off for Cotopaxi. On the morning of Saturday the group took a guided tour of the historic city centre while the five of us who had opted for the Cotopaxi adventure met Freddy Ramirez in his office. Freddy was then in his early thirties and impressed me right away as the kind of guy to whom you would entrust your life. He had spent a few years in Austria studying how to run a hotel and completing courses in mountain leadership. He spoke fluent German, French and English.

Our meeting had the purpose of discussing details of the arrangement and to hire climbing gear. Freddy expressed some doubt as to our chances of summiting such a big mountain after such a short time in the county. Quito is situated at almost 3,000 m above sea level and is the second highest capital in the world. Simply being there for a few days would help us to acclimatise. However, Freddy thought this would not suffice and advised us to climb *Rucu Pichincha*, the extinct volcano near Quito before attempting Cotopaxi.

The summit of Rucu Pichincha is 4,800 m above sea level, more or less the height of Mount Blanc. However, there is no snow or ice and the route is straightforward. Freddy's brother Emanuel could drive us in his jeep to the military post of Cruz Loma at 4,000 m. We could see that small peak from the city. It is easily recognised by the many antennas positioned on it. From there it was possible to hike to the top and back in five to six hours. We would not need a guide, as there are no navigation problems. It was possible to walk up to Cruz Loma but Freddy recommended to take his jeep for two reasons; firstly, to save time, and, secondly, because walking was not safe as one could be attacked by wild dogs or robbers. We agreed to his plan. Dr Tom asked him if it was a good idea to take tablets in order to speed up our acclimatization. Freddy's answer was absolutely unambiguous: Under no circumstances take tablets. They are all rubbish. The only way was proper acclimatisation. Freddy did not know that Dr Tom had started two days earlier dishing out tablets, which were supposed to prevent altitude sickness. As we had started taking the tablets, we felt that we had no choice but to continue. Naturally, we did not say anything about this to Freddy.

Early on Sunday morning at 9:00 o'clock Emanuel appeared with his jeep outside our hotel. When we had mentioned to the others in our group that we planned to drive to Cruz Loma and then hike to Rucu Pichincha they all got interested in walking at least part of the way towards the summit. We made a deal with Emanuel. First, he would take us five, plus whoever else might fit into his jeep. While we would do our hike, he would return to Quito and bring up the remainder of the group. In this way, everybody would get up to Cruz Loma and enjoy the view of the city from above.

The drive to Cruz Loma was horrendous. Nothing had prepared us for it. We knew, from the guidebooks, that the roads in Ecuador were often bad and could only be tackled with a four-wheel drive. But what we experienced was beyond our imagination. The route resembled a road only at the beginning of the drive. There was some asphalt, and higher up there were cobblestones. Soon the asphalt and cobblestones disappeared and gave way to a mixture of *lodo* (clay) and rocks. As it frequently rains, the clay was shaped into narrow riverbeds by the running water. Driving up Emanuel tried his best to straddle them. Sometimes the left or right wheels would fall into the riverbed making the car tilt dangerously to one side or the other. On occasion huge rocks were lying in the way. Going around them was not always possible. How we got *over* them I do not know. At times the road was extremely narrow. There were hairpin bends. The wheels of the car were worryingly close to the edge. We could see into an abyss down to the stony mass of Quito. At one stage Emanuel took a wrong turn. He tried to turn around and when he reversed, he almost went over the edge. I suggested timidly to him to reverse back to the turn-off rather than insist in trying to turn round. Luckily, he followed my advice. I was asking myself if it had not been better to walk all the way. Surely, the mad dogs and the robbers could not have posed any bigger danger than this so-called road!

When we finally got out of the jeep my knees were trembling. I took a few steps and had to sit down. At first, I thought that this was the consequence of the awful car ride. But I soon realised that it was the altitude that affected me. I had never been higher than 3,500 m. I was not the only one who felt the effect. Quite a few of the group got headaches, others vomited. Anyway, there we were and way down, 1,000 m beneath us we saw Quito. Most of the group started walking in the direction of the summit. Some decided to stay behind and enjoy the view, swallowing aspirin in order to ease their headaches. We five Cotopaxians wasted no time. As soon as we had gotten over the initial effects of the altitude we took off. In good Irish style we sprint-started. This is fine in Ireland where the highest elevation is 1,000 m above sea level and where one seldom climbs more than 400 m in one go. Here, in the Andes, a different approach is required. We had to continuously climb 800 m and we were starting at 4,000 m above sea level. The only sensible way to do this is to walk very slowly, taking literally one step at a time. At first it was not too bad. The incline was moderate enough and my headache disappeared.

There are two ridges leading up towards the summit. One of them starts from Cruz Loma. To our right was a deep valley. We could see across to another small peak that also contained a lot of antennas. From there the other ridge leads up towards the top of Rucu Pichincha. After walking a good hour we came to the point where the two ridges merged.

The ascent now became more strenuous. At first the path led along the right side the now very rocky mountain, then it turned left and went straight up to the summit. I began to feel the pressure in my head and fell behind. Pat Lynch and Dr Tom looked back but I waved to them to move on indicating that I would catch up. However, after a few minutes I realised that I could not continue any further. My head was now thumping and my stomach felt queasy. So, I decided to turn back. I arrived at the point where the two ridges united and continued towards the antennas. The city spread out in front of me. Now and then I had to sit down and drink some water. My head was sore and I felt sick to my stomach. After walking for a while, I got the distinct feeling that the way looked different from how I remembered it. I told myself that routes did not look the same when one walked them in the opposite direction. A few hikers came towards me. I had now completely forgotten the name of *Cruz Loma*. All I know was that there were antennas where the jeep had parked. So, I asked the hikers if this was *el camino por las antenas*. They all answered in the positive, which reassured me.

When I finally arrived at the antennas, I was delighted. My delight changed into panic when I realized that there were many more antennas than I remembered. There was no sign of Emanuel's jeep or of anybody of our group. Then I spotted a motorbike and close to it, in the grass, a courting couple. I looked to my right. Far away, across the deep valley, I saw the hill with a few antennas from where the other ridge leads up towards Rucu Pichincha. It now dawned on me that I had taken the wrong ridge! As I learned later, I was now standing on the little peak called *Las Antenas*. Like Cruz Loma, this was also a military post. When asking for the antennas I had been thinking of the antennas at *Cruz Loma*, but the locals I asked had naturally assumed that I wanted to go to the post called Las Antenas. It was now 4:00 p.m. It would be dark at half past six. There was no way I could get over to my friends on the other side of the valley who were, presumably, starting the search for their missing leader. What was I to do? I spotted a path leading in the direction of the airport. The only sensible thing was to descend via that path and then return by taxi to the hotel.

As I started walking, I saw a lone hiker coming up from that path. He was a young German who wanted to get to the top. I told him that this would take him at least two hours by which time it would be dark; he decided to go back the way he had come. I was delighted to have company. He was a student of geography working on his master's degree. He had been to Ecuador many times and spoke excellent Spanish. His thesis dealt with the Ecuadorian education system. As I did not see a connection between geography and education, I asked him to tell me more about it. He explained to me that due to the complex geography of the country, the extreme climatic conditions and the isolation of many villages in the Andes there were many communication problems. It proved very difficult to ensure an equal standard in all schools in as diverse places as the coast, the rainforest, the major cities and the Andes. In other words, the geographical situation was a factor hindering or, at least, complicating the development of a modern education system. Time passed pleasantly enough as we descended. My headache had disappeared completely and my energy had come back. I felt as if I could start climbing all over again.

When we reached the outskirts of the city, we waved down a taxi and asked the driver to bring us to the *Plaza de la Independencia*. There we both got out and said good-bye. He was interesting company and I would have liked to meet him again. However, this was not possible. I walked back to the hotel, which was only five minutes away. None of the group was there. Those who had come down from Rucu Pichincha were probably out drinking cocktails and dining while the others presumably were still searching for me on the mountain. There was nothing I could do. I took a shower and changed into respectable cloths. Then the hotel phone rang. It was Fidelma, who told me that they were still on Cruz Loma. The soldiers who manned the post had allowed her to use the phone. It was now getting dark very fast. Fidelma's voice sounded annoyed: "Do you realise that we have been looking for you for the past two hours?" I tried to tell her what had happened and that there had been no way I could have contacted them.

About an hour and a half later they arrived at the hotel and told me their version of events. When Emanuel drove part of the group back to Quito, Ursula and a few others stayed behind to wait for the five of us who had gone for the summit. When Pat, Dr Tom, Doreen and Ted arrived without me, Ursula anxiously asked about my whereabouts. They told her that they thought I would have been at Cruz Loma for some time, as I had descended earlier. Then panic set in. Two Ramblers, Dr Tom and Michael, literally ran back to the point where the two ridges joined up. Of course, there was no sign of a lost Herbert. At half past five Emanuel returned. He talked to the soldiers at Cruz Loma who phoned the military post at *Las Antenas*. They were told that a German who spoke good Spanish had been sighted. There was relief amongst the group because they thought that I was the "German" the soldiers at *Las Antenas* were referring to. Only when it materialised that the person in question was *joven* (young), it dawned on them that this could not be me. The *joven* was, of course, my German friend, the soldiers had met before I had bumped into him. The soldiers at Cruz Loma were extremely helpful and genuinely concerned. Two of them ran off into the fading light, in the direction of Rucu Pichincha, calling my name. A hang-glider who was getting ready to take off from Cruz Loma was asked to look for a lost *gringo*. It must have been quite dramatic.

The following morning, Freddy and his crew picked us up to drive to Cotopaxi. When we told him of our adventure, he was highly amused. It was not a good omen if *el jefe* lost his way on the very first Andean ascent.

Our attempt to reach the summit of Cotopaxi failed. After having done about two thirds of the route the weather turned seriously bad and we were forced to return.

7.3 Guayaquil 1995

The same trip to Ecuador, in the summer of 1995 with our Irish friends also led us to Otavalo, Cuenca, La Amazonia, Guayaquil and to the Galapagos Islands. After having returned from the Galapagos, our friends flew back to Ireland and Ursula and myself stayed another ten days in the country.

I had an invitation from the German School in Guayaquil to deliver a lecture on Johann Nestroy, an Austrian playwright of the 19th century, to a class of high school students. The Head of the German School put us up in his house in an elegant suburb of the city. Most houses in the neighbourhood were secured with heavy gates inside of which one could hear the mighty barks of Mastiffs, Dobermans or Rottweilers. It was not uncommon to see armed guards outside the gates. Our host had neither a guard dog nor an armed guard. His house was comfortable and spacious and had a swimming pool.

The German school was situated in a big park, with all kinds of exotic trees under which I spotted a few Iguanas. It was a fee-paying school only the moneyed elite could afford. The students were friendly and well behaved. A power failure occurred in the middle of my lecture and the windowless classroom was plunged into darkness. Candles were brought in and the class was continued in romantic candlelight. The PowerPoint programme and the pictures I had prepared were of no further use. Similar power failures had happened in the past few days all over the country due to technical problems at one of the country's biggest hydroelectric power stations. I was told that the problem was bad maintenance.

In the evening, following my lecture, the Head of the German School invited Ursula and myself to dinner in an elegant restaurant. Some of the teachers were also there. The clientele was made up of the kind of people, who might be prone to be targeted by robbers and kidnappers. One of the teachers told us a story, which he swore was true and had happened a few months ago in that very restaurant. Armed robbers entered the establishment, ordered everybody to put up their hands and then searched the handbags and pockets of the customers for money. They also took the women's jewellery. One lady had the presence of mind to quickly drop her gold chain into her soup where it remained well hidden until the robbers left the restaurant.

The next morning, we strolled around the city. We came to the harbour and watched the loading of a freight ship. There was no crane. Instead, a ramp led from the quay onto the ship. The incline of the ramp was at least 15%. Heavy bags (no idea what was in them) were placed on the backs of strong men who ran up the ramp and threw the bags onto the deck of the ship. They had to run very fast, it was most important that they kept up the momentum. If anyone had lost momentum he would have fallen down or lost the bag half way up. It was fascinating to see a system in operation that still used physical labour instead of machinery. Obviously physical labour was extremely cheap in Ecuador.

Before returning to Quito and flying back to Ireland we spent a few days in a simple hotel on a beach, not too far from Guayaquil. Unfortunately, I have forgotten the name of the area. It was low season; the sky was grey but the temperature was around a pleasant 30° C. We were the only tourists. The beach was a working beach where men were collecting larvae of shrimps, which they sold to shrimp farms. The men were standing all day up to their waist in the water collecting tiny larvae. They were lucky if a day's labour yielded a small bucket that would make them five dollars. Instead of leaving the larvae in their natural environment they were fished out and brought into an artificial setting so that more shrimps could be produced. Most of the shrimps were exported to the United States, where the demand for this delicacy is insatiable.

One day the chef showed us a big lobster that had been freshly caught. He offered to prepare it for us, which we gladly accepted. The only downside was that the hotel had no wine. We drank beer instead. This was not ideal but the lobster was delicious.

7.4 Lost on Cotopaxi 2001

It was 10.30 at night on 28th January 2001. Everybody in the hut was fast asleep as the three of us, Mary R, Patricia and myself, struggled down the creaky wooden stairs, into the kitchen doing our best not to wake anybody up. The temperature outside was about minus 10° C. The Refugio José Ribas is 4,800 m above sea level and about three hundred metres below the mighty glacier of Cotopaxi. Most climbers start around midnight and try to reach the summit at sunrise, so that they can get off the glacier before the snow gets too soft, in the hot Ecuadorian sun. We had decided to attempt summiting without the help of guides, and we reckoned that an extra early start might give us some leeway in case we got into difficulties. Climbing and hiking in the Ecuadorian Andes requires starting at unholy hours.

Getting to the hut had been a bit of an adventure. For the past week or so there had been strikes all over the country. The indigenous population was protesting against rising costs and worsening living standards. In many areas they set up roadblocks that made travelling an unpredictable business. One never knew how long it would take to get to one's destination and if one would be able to return to where one came from. We had ordered a taxi that was to bring us to the car park 200 m below the refuge and to pick us up from there the following day between 2:00 and 3:00 p.m.

At two o'clock in the afternoon the driver arrived at our hotel in Quito. We had agreed on a price of hundred dollars for the round trip. The driver had assured us that he knew the way, as he had brought up people to the refuge *muchas veces*, many times. It soon became obvious, however, that he had never been there before. Luckily, we knew the way and could direct him. We arrived at the gate of the National Park at 4:00 p.m., too late to enter as the gate-keeper informed us. After some negotiation he let us pass but impressed on the driver that he must be out of the park by 6:00 p.m. After that the gate would be locked.

So, on we drove up the winding and bumpy road towards the refuge. At every turn the worried driver asked us ¿*Ya está el refugio*? He was visibly disappointed when we told him that this was only a tool shed or a shelter for animals. The road got worse and the driver started seriously worrying about his car. Half an hour's walk from the car park he stopped and refused to continue. We had no choice but to walk the remainder of the way. Before leaving us, he asked for part of the money. We said that we would pay him tomorrow when he had brought us back to the hotel. However, he argued that he needed to buy petrol to get home. We gave him twenty dollars. The rest he would get tomorrow. We genuinely were in no position to give him more. For security reasons we had taken little cash with us. We hoped that we had enough left to pay for the hut.

As we were plodding towards the refuge with our heavy backpacks it began to snow. We got there at 5:30 p.m. and found that we did not have enough money to pay for the accommodation. I tried my best to explain the situation to the two young hut wardens, Miguel and Sergio. They kindly let us get away with five dollars less than we ought to pay. We promised to send them the money via one of Freddy's guides who came up regularly. We cooked our simple meals, some instant rice and pasta dishes, which we had brought from Ireland, tea and a few bars of chocolate and went to bed by seven o'clock in the vain hope of getting some sleep. Even a few sleepless hours of resting are better than nothing.

A group of Americans entered the dormitory half an hour later. They took forever to settle in their bunk beds. When all was finally quiet, one of their party started to cough and to breathe heavily. He obviously suffered badly from altitude sickness. He groaned and turned in his bed, got up every few minutes looking for something or other in his haversack. There was a constant rustle of plastic bags. Then he began to talk to himself (or to somebody of his party): "Where is my toilet paper? Somebody has stolen my toilet paper! These f…. people have taken my toilet paper…" He continued in this vein for another half hour before he finally shut up.

At 10.30 p.m. Mary's alarm went off and we got up. The snow conditions were supposed to be better than in the previous days, so one of the wardens had told us. We gobbled down our breakfast, hot coffee and some biscuits, put on our harnesses and walked into the darkness. There was no moon. However, as there were no clouds either and the stars were out in all their glory, our eyes soon adjusted and we could walk without switching on our head torches. Ahead of us we could see the silhouette of the mountain. I had my compass ready but had to look at it only once in a while. After an hour and a half, we reached the glacier. It took us some time to find the start of the route. I had been here in 1997 with a few Irish friends when we successfully summited with the help of Freddy Ramirez. Of course, the glacier looked different now from how I remembered it.

After searching for a few minutes, we discovered footsteps, which appeared to go in the right direction. We roped up, switched on our torches and started moving, avoiding a crevasse here and a sheer drop there, crossing snow bridges, jumping over small crevasses etc. As we got higher the ground got steeper and the snow became knee deep, which made walking very tiresome. By three o'clock in the morning we reached a flat and sheltered spot where we rested. We were about three hours away from the summit. In two hours, we would reach *Yanasacha*. This is a Quechuan word and means black wall. This huge rock face is visible from many miles away. It is black because due to its steepness it remains permanently free of snow. There one has to turn right and move for one hour along a narrow shoulder to the summit.

Our route continued over more steep ground and in deep snow. After an hour and half of tough going we met a group that came towards us. Their guide told us that they had been as far as Yanasacha and had to give up. There was no way they could reach the summit, as the snow was too deep. Although this did not sound good, we went on for another fifteen minutes and then stopped and reassessed our situation. As we were doing this, another group came towards us. They, too, had given up. We did not see any point in continuing. We were exhausted from the fight against the deep snow. We had made a valiant attempt and felt it was wise to turn back. Later we found out that nobody had summited that day. So, we had made the right decision.

It was now close to 5:00 a.m. I had led all the way up; Patricia was second and Mary third on the rope. Now, descending, Mary was first and I at the back. We slowly meandered downhill, first the not so steep bit, then left down the very steep incline to the sheltered flat spot. From there the route got somewhat complicated, leading between huge crevasses and over some dramatic ice bridges. By about 6:00 a.m. it got brighter. Just as the sun was trying to break through a heavy mist descended. Although it was now bright, we could see nothing. Everything was white. We followed the footsteps as well as we could and consulted the compass more often. Suddenly we saw no more footsteps. We looked around, retraced a bit, still no footsteps. Visibility was down to about ten metres. It was impossible to know where we were. It began to dawn on us that we were lost. It was 7:00 a.m.

It was a weird feeling. None of us had ever been lost on a really big mountain before. Getting lost in Ireland is no big deal. The maps of the Irish mountains are very detailed. Even if he has lost his bearings an experienced hill-walker can establish, fairly safely, his whereabouts with the help of a map and a compass. And one is never too far away from civilisation. Sooner or later, one is bound to hit a road. This however, was a very big mountain, very far away from civilisation. If we could not find the hut, we would not find shelter. The Ecuadorian maps are far less precise than the Irish ones. The 1:50,000 maps of the Irish mountains show contours every ten metres thus providing quite a good idea of how the land lies. The contours on the Ecuadorian maps of the same scale are forty metres apart. It is far more difficult to get an image of the terrain from them. It felt very strange, but none of us panicked. We knew that we could not be too far from the correct path. We had to keep calm and not move further away.

We moved down a little. There was a miniature valley on our left across which we could not see. On our right the ground seemed to rise, moving down the ground got steeper. Then the fog lifted a bit. Looking down in the direction where our compass pointed the ground was falling at a very steep angle and huge crevasses appeared. We had no desire to get too close to them and decided to move back up. The miniature valley on our right (on our left when looking downhill) seemed to narrow as we went uphill, which indicated that another shoulder might merge further up with the one we were on. Mary was now in front and I was last. I put my ice axe into the ground and got a shock when I realized that underneath the few inches of hard snow there was a void. We were right over a crevasse. We must get out of this as quickly as possible. I shouted to Mary to set up an anchor and take us on a tight rope. We soon got out of danger and looked around. I figured that our route would have to be towards our left as we looked downhill. Suddenly Patricia, looking in the direction I pointed, shouted: "I can see the track!" She was right. We finally reached what was clearly the track we had lost. We had moved too far to the right and had started to climb down another spur.

It was now 10.30 a.m. We had eaten nothing since we left the hut at 11:00 p.m., and drunk nothing since 5:00 a.m. It was still bitter cold and we found it almost impossible to open our rucksacks as the zips and straps were frozen. We managed to eat some chocolate, swallow a few drops of cold water and then moved on. The fog continued to lift, and half an hour later we could see the refuge. We reached it at 11.30 a.m. What a relieve this was!

We were totally iced up and looked like a party just having descended from Mount Everest. We took photographs of each other and then began to take off our gear. The two young hut wardens, Miguel and Sergio, helped us. Very expertly they coiled our ropes. Sergio took one of my ice axes and made some graceful swinging movements with it. They seemed to have experience with climbing equipment and I presumed that they had climbed all the big mountains of their country. Miguel said that he was from the Cayambe region. I told him that we had climbed Cayambe only ten days ago and asked him if he had been up there too. To our surprise he answered in the negative. Not only had he and Sergio not climbed Cayambe, they had never been on the top of Cotopaxi either. When I asked why not, he said that they could not afford the equipment. I felt ashamed for having asked such a stupid and insensitive question.

At twelve o'clock we left the hut and made for the car park. From there we continued downhill for another two hundred metres, to the point where our driver had stopped and promised to pick us up. There was no sign of him. After waiting for an hour, we feared the worst. He would not be coming back! We stood under one of those shelters, which the taxi driver had taken to be the refuge. I began to look for alternative transport. We had noticed a few cars at the car park. Hopefully, one of them would have room for us and drive us down. I stopped a car moving up towards the car park below the refuge. The driver told me that he would come back by five o'clock and that he would be able to take us if our taxi had not have appeared by then. It was a long time to wait but it gave us some consolation. After half an hour another car was driving down. I waved it down, but there was no room for us. We decided to go back to the car park. Maybe there was a driver in one of the cars there and we could make a deal. When we got there, we saw only empty cars. Disheartened we started to descend again towards the spot where the taxi driver had refused to continue driving. To our great surprise our taxi was there! We were never so pleased to see a taxi as in that moment. By five o'clock in the afternoon we were back in our hotel in Quito. We paid the balance of the fare and gave the driver a good tip on top of the agreed price. All's well that ends well.

7.5 The Avenue of the Volcanoes; Baños around 2000

A travel guidebook of the time described Ecuador as one of the politically, economically and geologically most unstable countries of South America. As far as politics are concerned, this was an exaggeration. True, Ecuador, like most other Latin American countries, has had her share of military takeovers and dictatorships. However, in the past decades it has been one of the better functioning democracies of the continent. In spite of this the economy is not doing well. Statistics rank Ecuador amongst the poorest nations of South America. I have seen districts of Quito and of Ecuador's largest city, Guayaquil on the Pacific coast, where people live in appalling poverty.

Nevertheless, it must be said that although there is plenty of poverty in the big cities, the indigenous population of the Andes lives relatively well. Land reforms in the 1960s have done away with the big *latifundia* whose tenant peasants could hardly scrape a living. Most farmers now own their own land and feed themselves. The indigenous people who live in the Andes and cultivate their fields of maize and potatoes on incredibly steep ground in altitudes of up to 4,000 m may appear poor to us, but they are well fed and well clad. They produce much of their own food and make most of their own cloths. Many make a good enough living by selling their food, textiles and crafts on the various markets.

The biggest of the indigenous markets is in Otavalo, a town some 80 km north of the capital Quito. The natives of Otavalo have developed an excellent marketing system. Their hats, pullovers, bags, rugs, ponchos and other products are sold not only all over Ecuador but also in many other South American countries. When we travelled in Chile, we noticed that the best pullovers, the finest rugs with the best design, the most original smoking pipes and children's toys sold in the markets there came, almost without exception from Ecuador, which meant in most cases from Otavalo.

What is truly unstable in Ecuador is the geology. In this respect the guidebook was correct. Earthquakes and volcanic eruptions are quite common. However, this is by no means an Ecuadorian speciality. The traveller may encounter natural disturbances of this kind anywhere in Central- or South America. In her novel *La casa de los espíritus* (*The House of the Spirits*) Isabel Allende describes Chile as *un país de catastrofes*, a land of catastrophes.

Three days after arriving in Santiago de Chile in December 1997 Ursula and myself experienced a slight earthquake. We were having our breakfast when the lamp above our table suddenly began to sway to and fro and the crockery in the sideboard made a tinkling noise. Our hosts in this private bed and breakfast did not bat an eyelid. This, they said reassuringly, was quite normal, it happened every few weeks, no need to panic. All the houses in Santiago were built to withstand earthquakes.

We had experienced our very first earthquake two and a half years earlier in Baños, in Ecuador. That attractive little town is situated a four-hour bus ride southeast of Quito, at the rim of the Amazonian basin. The houses nestle between the 5,023 m high volcano *Tungurahua* and the deep gorge of the River Pastaza, which contributes to the huge network of waterways that eventually find their way into the majestic Amazonas. At the foot of the volcano are two hot springs that have been tapped and channelled into hot baths.

No wonder that the whole area is a potential death trap. One might be swallowed up by the earth or suffocated by ash rain or buried by lava flow. Nothing that dramatic happened to us. One night, however, we were kept awake by the howling of dogs. All of a sudden, the floor began to vibrate and we heard a sound as if somebody was trying to move the furniture. The whole episode lasted only a few seconds. It occurred to us that we had just experienced an earthquake. Next morning some of our group mentioned that they had they same experience.

Is it too far-fetched to draw a connection between the geological and the political instability of the Andean states? Isabel Allende certainly does not think so. In her largely autobiographical work *Paula*, she writes:

> In Chile we are influenced (*determinados*) by the eternal presence of the mountains that separate us from the rest of the continent, and by a sense of precariousness inevitable in a region of geological and political catastrophes. Everything trembles beneath our feet; we know no security. If anyone asks us how we are, we answer "About the same" (*sin novedad*), or "All right, I guess (*más o menos*)." We move from one uncertainty to another; we pick our way through a twilight region. Nothing is precise. We do not like confrontations. We prefer to negotiate. When circumstances push us to extremes, our worst instincts are awakened and history takes a tragic turn, because the same men who seem mild-mannered in their everyday lives can, if offered impunity and the right pretext, turn into bloodthirsty beasts

The analogy that Allende draws between the geological and political catastrophes of her country may seem somewhat 'poetic', but it is tempting. The Andes are young mountains. Their formation is still going on with all the turbulence this causes. The Andean states are also politically young. Their borders and their social fabric are still in the process of consolidation. Neither has the crust of the earth cooled down and hardened nor has social fermentation ceased. With the exception of what formerly was Yugoslavia, Europe appears to have put these processes largely behind her. I am talking here of perceptions, rather than of realities. We know that perceptions can influence reality and it seems fair to say that the process of political and geological consolidation, from which present-day Europe is benefitting, is far from completed in South America. When Alexander von Humboldt called the valley between the two cordilleras of the Andes, running through Ecuador from north to south the "Avenue of the Volcanoes" he referred to the geology of the area. However, he created a suitable metaphor for the political, social and economic instability that has plagued so many Andean states for so long.

On both sides of the Pan-American Highway, that runs through Ecuador, seldom more than twenty of thirty kilometres away, loom the gigantic volcanoes. Many are active but have not posed any threat for some time. Next to Quito is Rucu Pichincha and a bit further west Guagua Pichincha. Like most of the names of these mountains, these are Quechuan names. "Rucu" Pichincha is the "old" and "Guagua" Pichincha the "young" Pinchincha. While the old one is extinct, the young one is very active. I climbed the young one in the summer of 1998 and looked into the crater, which was filled with a mixture of mist and vapours so I could not see to the bottom. There was no rumbling, no fire, only a faint scent of sulphur. However, a few months later it began to rumble and throw hot rocks at an unsuspecting climbing party. Quito was put on yellow alert. About a year later the rumblings became very noticeable and at night one could see a red glow. The capital was put on red alert. Finally, in 2000 Guagua Pichincha erupted violently creating a mushroom cloud as high and spectacular like that caused by a nuclear explosion. The column of smoke went some thirty kilometres up into the atmosphere. A huge rain of ash fell on Quito and covered everything.

Some sixty kilometres south of Quito, to the east of the Pan-American Highway is Cotopaxi. In the 20th century it erupted in 1903 and 1904 and then again in 1942. After half a century of no activity it began to warm up again and broke out in 2015. Further south, to the West of the highway is the highest mountain of Ecuador, Chimborazo. "Chimbo" as the mountain guides lovingly call it, is believed to be extinct, although some volcanologists are not completely sure about it. Still further south is Sangay, Ecuador's most dramatically active volcano. It erupts continuously and spectacularly. Some mad people climb it, but the mountain guides refuse to go beyond a certain point because it is too dangerous. If some crazy *gringos* have a death wish, they are welcome to enjoy the thrill!

The place I associate most with volcanic activities is the small and charming town of Baños on the edge of the Amazon basin, approximately four hours by bus from Quito. At Ambato, some hundred and fifty kilometres south of Quito, the bus leaves the Pan American Highway turning east and descends to Baños. The town nestles at the foot of snow-capped volcano Tungurahua, the source of hot springs that are channelled into various pools. (Baños means baths). The temperature of the water emanating from the springs ranges from 26 to 50° C.

One good reason to visit Baños is that from there one can travel by bus, by jeep bicycle right down to the rainforest of El Oriente or La Amazonia. The road (if one can call it that) runs alongside the Rio Pastaza, which ultimately joins the network of rivers feeding the Amazonas.

> The beautifully formed cone of Tungurahua, whose peak is always white looks as if God had let it fall out of His hand into the eastern cordillera of the Andes, where the impact created a broad base in its

bowels. In the gorge at the feet of this colossus that rises out of such depth to a height of 5,087 m above sea level the River Pastaza is formed by the joining together of the Patate, which is watering the province of Tungurahua in the East, with the Chambo River that has made its way through the province of Chimborazo. From here the newly formed river thunders downhill through rock and lava (…)

Further downriver of the Agoyán waterfall, whose noise can be heard over long distances, one hour on foot from the pretty rural town of Baños, this new river takes on the name of Pastaza. Violent rapids frequently interrupt its majestic flow. Of the many tributaries that feed it, the most important are the Verde and Topo rivers. (…)

The River Pastaza, one of the kings of the water systems of the East, which ultimately unite themselves with the supreme monarch, the Amazonas (…) has the most wonderful landscapes by its banks (…)

This is how in 1879 the Ecuadorian writer Juan Leon Mera described the formation of the River Pastaza near Baños in his novel *Cumandá*.

Ursula and I visited Baños for the first time in August 1995 with our friends from the Irish Ramblers and Wayfarers. We did not use it as the starting point for our tour of the rainforest as we had spent five days in the jungle the previous week, having flown there from Quito. We wanted to spend some time in Baños because the guide books recommended it as a pleasant spa resort, where one can relax in the hot springs, go horse riding, eat well and recover from altitude sickness. The town lies only 1,800 m above sea level.

We could not resist the temptation to follow the road alongside the Rio Pastaza towards the rainforest of La Amazonia or El Oriente. So, one day we hired mountain bikes and descended as far as we could in one day. Our destination was the town of Mera. We figured that we could get there and back in one day. In the summer of 1995, the route to Mera was only partly a road. For long stretches it was covered by gravel or, even worse, by clay. In the hot equatorial sun the clay turns to dust. Whenever a bus or lorry whisked by, we were covered in it. Thank God it did not rain. When the clay gets wet, it becomes a sea of mud. As we were descending the cycling was easy enough. We had to be careful not to be pushed into the river by passing vehicles. The further down we went, the warmer it became and the vegetation changed. There were orange groves near the road and banana trees surrounded the villages. Locals had set up stalls and sold oranges and bananas to the passers-by. Occasionally we had to cycle through rivers that crossed the road or to duck under waterfalls.

Soon after crossing the Rio Verde we arrived at the village of the same name. It consisted of a few shacks and a restaurant. The restaurant building was a shack too. As we were hungry we threw caution to the winds and decided to have something to eat. The place certainly did not look hygienic, but we figured that after three weeks in the country our tummies had adjusted sufficiently to the local bacteria. The soup I ate tasted delicious. Some of our friends chose stews of obscure composition. Nobody got ill. Maybe the kitchen was cleaner than we assumed or we had, indeed, adjusted to the bacteria of Ecuador. After lunch the majority of the group decided that they had done enough cycling and opted for returning to Baños. They hoped that there would be enough time to visit one of the two hot spas before dinner. A few of us, including myself, wished to go a bit further. We went as far as Rio Negro and Puyo. Mera turned out to be too far.

Before we moved on, we watched our friends getting on the bus. The good thing about cycling from Baños towards La Amazonia is that one does not have to cycle back uphill. There are plenty of buses that stop anywhere and transport bikes on the roof. The public transport system of Ecuador is excellent and deserves to be praised. Within a few minutes of waiting a bus came along. It stopped and our crowd handed their bikes to the driver's assistant who had climbed onto the roof of the bus in order to haul the bikes up and secure them. Suddenly a second bus appeared and also stopped. Part of our crowd who were waiting for their bikes to be taken went to the second bus. I noticed that the fellow on the roof of the first bus showed unmistakable signs of being displeased when half of his customers defected to the other bus. The second bus was loaded quicker and took off before the first bus. I had a premonition that things might not be too pleasant and I was right.

When we arrived in Baños later in the afternoon, Ursula told me what happened. She was in the bus that had stopped first. The driver was furious because he had lost half his customers to the competition, which, to make things worse, was now ahead. When the bikes had finally been secured on his roof, he took off in a great hurry. Obviously, his intention was to catch up with and overtake the bus ahead of him. He had pulled away so suddenly that his assistant had no time to get back into the bus. He was now on the roof hanging on for dear life. The road was narrow. On the right were the slopes of the mountains and on the left the gorge of the Pastaza. The slopes on the right were steep, often rocky, sometimes slightly overhanging. When the bus got too close to the right its side scratched the shrubs and, sometimes, the rocks. After a while the driver succeeded in overtaking the bus in front of him. In doing so he came dangerously close to the abyss at the bottom of which the river was gushing down towards the jungle. Soon the other bus overtook him again. A mad race between the two drivers developed. It was a miracle that neither of the two buses plunged into the river.

There were American tourists on the bus who told Ursula that this caper was a regular feature and that so far this year five buses had fallen into the gorge. The most astonishing thing was the reaction of the indigenous people travelling on that bus. They did not react at all. They sat on their seats stony faced. It was impossible to detect any fear, anger, surprise or any other emotion. It appeared that all this nonsense had nothing whatsoever to do with them. The fact that their lives were put at risk did not seem to worry them.

For the *andinista* Baños is the ideal place to relax after the effort of climbing big mountains. It is a good place to recover from altitude sickness and rest tired limbs in the hot sulphur baths. My favourite bath was *El Salado* a bit outside the town in the direction of Ambato. It had several pools at different temperatures, as well as a cold pool under a waterfall from which one could get a shoulder massage. At the entrance were stalls that sold fresh sugar cane, cane juice and grilled bananas. Every five to ten minutes a shuttle bus went between the spa and the town.

There are numerous good restaurants in the town. We frequented *Düsseldorf*, which in spite of its name did not, as I had feared, serve only *Eisbein and Sauerkraut* but offered pasta and shellfish, good soups, exotic fruit salads and other specialities of the country. Another favourite restaurant of mine was *El Marques* where they served an excellent ceviche (a fish soup made of raw fish that has been marinated for a few hours in lime juice), and good steaks, and where live music almost always was found. I also have good memories of *El Higueron* that had been recommended to me by my friend Freddy. It was a small and cosy place with a limited menu, but the food was freshly cooked and well worth waiting for. We discovered a cocktail bar in the main street that had never heard of a closing hour. It was on the first floor and one could sit all day and night on the balcony overlooking the busy street, while sipping cocktails. In this place, like in many other restaurants all over the country, the bartender knew how to make cocktails. He did not open bottles with ready mixes, but prepared the cocktails from fresh ingredients in a professional manner.

Baños lives from tourism and it lives well out of it. I returned there in 1997 and in 1998. Each time we stayed in the *Hotel Flor de Oriente* beside the town park. My fond memories suffered a shock in the summer of 1999 when I read that Tungurahua had, quite unexpectedly, erupted seriously and that the town had been evacuated. Only a few months earlier Guagua Pichincha had erupted near Quito – and now this! The situation was obviously dangerous. Ecuadorian newspapers showed pictures of the empty streets of Baños being patrolled by soldiers, who were there to prevent the inhabitants from returning against the order of the authorities and, presumably, to protect the town against looters.

On 3rd April 2000 I received a surprise fax from the owner of the Hotel Flor de Oriente:

Dear Mr. Herzmann

I am writing to you first, to ask how you are and, secondly, to tell you a little about our situation. As you probably know we have had a difficult time due to the eruption of the volcano Tungurahua. Our town was completely evacuated for three months. During that time, we could not work, but, thanks to God, nothing happened to the town. On the first of January 2000 all of us who had been evacuated decided to return to Baños. We had to fight the Army, which tried to prevent our return. Since then, we are here and, slowly, our business is picking up again.

We have now one tourist attraction more. The daily eruptions of the volcano are continuing. At night one can see the glowing rocks which the crater hurls many miles into the sky. During the day huge pillars of steam and ash can be seen which reach a height of up to 10,000 m.

Volcanologists are monitoring the situation and we have emergency plans. Occasionally we carry out evacuation exercises in which all the population and tourists take part.

I hope you will visit us again this year and have the opportunity to see this natural phenomenon which occurs only every eighty years or so.

Looking forward to hearing from you.

I immediately faxed them my address and within a few weeks a letter arrived with stunning photos of Tungurahua in action. I decided to go back to Ecuador as soon as possible.

In January 2001, I returned to Ecuador with two friends from my Irish hiking clubs. One was Mary R from the Wayfarers, the other was Patricia from the Ramblers. Patricia's ambition then was to climb Mount Everest. Her trip to Ecuador was to prepare her for that. After climbing Imbabura and unsuccessful attempts at Cotacachi and Cotopaxi we felt it was time to relax and took the bus to Baños. We checked into the Hotel Flor de Oriente. The owner was there, she recognised me right away and welcomed me with signs of great affection. It felt like coming home. It was raining heavily. It was only half past four, too early to search for a restaurant and too late to pay a visit to El Salado. So, we went to the cocktail bar in the main street with the balcony from where one could watch the world go by. Mary and I ordered *una margarita* each, while Patricia ordered a *piña colada* without alcohol. There we were, sitting on the balcony, looking up at the rainy mountains and down into the busy main street. Tungurahua was invisible. We did not hear any rumbling noises either. We were later informed that the activity had more or less ceased. However, it was still forbidden to climb it.

Next morning, I met the owner's brother. He had gained weight since I had last seen him. Instead of the motorbike that he had been riding two years before he now drove a smart four-wheel drive Jeep. He showed no visible signs of the trials and tribulations he, like everybody else in this town, must have gone through. That also applied to the physical appearance of the town. It seemed in good nick, even cleaner and smarter than I remembered it. The brother told me about the hard times they had gone through. For three months everybody had to be put up by friends or relatives in other parts of the country. The government did not (and, I should think, could not afford to) pay for accommodation for all evacuees. The soldiers, who were supposed to guard the town and protect the property of the inhabitants, stole whatever they could find. And needless to say, no compensation was paid for the losses that everybody suffered. I had no reason to doubt what I was told. However, I had reason to be impressed by the speedy recovery of the town and the remarkable resilience of the inhabitants.

The activities of the volcano are both, a curse and a blessing for the town. The hot baths, which are said to have healing qualities, owe their existence to the volcano and are the main reason why tourists go there. The interior walls of the church are covered by paintings that tell stories about the volcano and the hot springs and, most importantly, about the miracles worked by *La Virgen de Las Aguas Santas* (the Virgin of the Holy Waters). Underneath each painting is a written explanation of what it depicts. Most of the pictures have to do with the volcano and all of them relate to miracles ascribed to the Virgin. Two paintings show the big fire in Guayaquil at the beginning of the 20th century. A whole street burnt down then. Only one house was spared. Its owner remembered that he had a picture of *La Virgen de Las Aguas Santas* of Baños. He managed to fetch it from where it was hidden and to pray to it. His prayer was heard, and the flames miraculously bypassed his house. At the beginning of the 18th century a procession took place. The statue of the Virgin was solemnly carried around. All of a sudden, the volcano began to thunder and to throw up flames. Understandably, the population panicked fearing the worst. Suddenly the statue moved. It raised the right hand and made an appeasing gesture to Tungurahua, which immediately quietened down. Another story, not related to the volcano, is about a man who crossed the River Pastaza to get into the town from the mountains on the northern side. There was no proper bridge, only a kind of hand powered cable car. He had to pull the cable to get the small *carro* in which he sat while crossing the river. Unfortunately, the cable broke and the man fell into the river. As he was falling, he called out aloud *Virgen de las Aguas Santas*, and lo and behold, the next moment he felt himself being gripped by an invisible hand and pulled out of the rapid river to safety on the bank.

The biggest miracle the volcano has worked in conjunction with the Virgin are the *Aguas Santas*, the holy and hot springs. The original springs are not the ones from El Salado that I liked to frequent but are at a waterfall in the middle of the town. They figure in many of the paintings in the church. Since I had never been there before, I suggested visiting them. The baths in the town are much smaller than El Salado and do not offer the great variety of pools of different temperature, neither can they boast a waterfall for a shower, nor the stunning view into the mountains.

The events of 1999 and 2000 are no less miraculous than the devout stories of the 18th and 19th centuries. The inhabitants know how to turn the threat of the volcano into a blessing. A few weeks after having arrived back home in Ireland I received the following email:

It is friends like you that make our work so satisfactory. We are very happy to count you and your friends amongst our regular guests. We would like to tell you now about our carnival, which we celebrated. We had so many tourists that there was not enough room for them in all the hotels. This is, of course, very good for our economy, which, as you know has suffered severely due to the biggest crisis in the history of our town. We trust in God that He may help us to stay in Baños. May He make sure that the volcano will not do further damage to us.

Dear friend, in the name of us here in the hotel Flor de Oriente, we send you our cordial greetings and hope that we will remain in contact.

I am already looking forward to my next visit to Baños.

7.6 Ethnic diversity

While Ursula was fearing for her life in the bus racing the narrow road from Rio Verde to Baños she could not help noticing the stoic *indigenas* who appeared to be completely unperturbed by the madness. They were sitting stony faced in their seats. It was impossible to tell what they felt or if they felt anything at all. This stoicism is typical of them. Whatever might happen, they take everything in their stride. Motionless they squat on the pavement beside their stalls in the market. If a customer wants to buy something, fine, if nobody stops to look at what they have to sell, this is also fine. They just sit and wait. It is as if they go into a kind of waiting mode, a bit like a computer. Obviously, they are not completely switched off, because they can return to full activity in a split second when a customer shows interest in their goods. But in this waiting mode they can remain for hours and hours.

In the summer of 1998 we were camping at the foot of Chimborazo. The camp was over 4,000 m above sea level. Close by were a few thatched cottages of indigenous families. All they had were a few llamas and fields on incredibly steep slopes, where they grew maize and potatoes. Their huts were extremely small, like those in the West of Ireland in pre-famine times. The word of our arrival spread quickly. We were a group of fifteen *gringos* led by Freddy Ramirez and his guide Abram who, we hoped, would bring us up to the summit of Chimborazo. As the weather was atrocious, we did not make it. We did not even try. Instead we attempted to reach the peak of the smaller *Carihuairazo*, a 5,000 m high extinct volcano just beside "Chimbo".

As we did not succeed with this either due to the bad weather, we were hanging around our tents a lot. It was not long until the locals appeared. At first a few women and their children showed up and busied themselves doing something or other in the fields nearby. We could not see what they were doing. I suspect, all they did was wait. We were waiting for the weather to clear and they were waiting for us to show an interest in what they had to sell. Never did they openly approach us. To actively go after the customer is simply not done in Ecuador. One can go to a market, look at the goods, take them or leave them without the harassment one has to put up with in India or in Arab countries. The women and their children just stayed in the nearby fields, most of the time they were just sitting there without moving. One morning we went for a hike in the rain. The *indigenas* were sitting at some distance from the tents. When we came back by lunchtime they were still sitting there, for all we could tell they had not changed their position. When we finally approached them they happily moved up to our tents and showed us handmade bags, shawls and other items. We bought everything. Their patience had paid off.

The *indigenas* count for roughly a quarter of Ecuador's population. Between 7% and 10% are black, and 10% are of white European stock. The rest are *mestizos*, a mixture of whites and indigenous people. The Afro-Ecuadorians live on the coast near the city of Esmeraldas and are the descendants of slaves who were brought there centuries ago.

Amongst other ethnic minorities the Lebanese play an important role. Many are leaders of the business community and also active in politics. One of the best-known and most controversial political figures was Abdalá Jaime Bucaram Ortiz who became president of Ecuador in 1996. He was a wealthy man and had made an impression as an entertainer and pop singer. He then tried his hand at politics. During the election campaign he made outrageous statements. His main opponent's sperm count, Bucaram alleged, was far inferior to his. Obviously, this kind of macho talk helped to secure him his victory. Once in power he promoted his pop records. Now that everybody knew him, he hoped to sell more. In a very short time, he succeeded in running the already weak economy completely into the ground. His abilities as an entertainer helped for a while to distract from the looming economic disaster. He caught the attention of the world press when he publicly honoured an Ecuadorian woman who lived in the United States and had cut off her husband's penis while he was asleep. The husband was rushed to hospital and the cut off piece was sown back. I do not recall if the press reported on the degree of success of that operation. Bucaram received that woman in the presidential palace in Quito and declared that she had done Ecuador proud. No wonder he became known amongst the Ecuadorian people by the nickname of *el loco*, the madman.

When he had finished ruining the economy, he tried to save it by introducing drastic increases of the prices of basic commodities. This led to violent protests. Bucaram was seen to join the protesters to all appearances supporting their demands against the measures of the government of which he was the head. When things became untenable Parliament finally ousted him. This was done by using an ancient piece of legislation that allowed for deposing of a head of state on grounds of mental instability. Maybe the United States should have learned from Ecuador when Donald Trump was president. Before Bucaram left the country as a political fugitive for Panama he plundered the national treasury. This seemed to be easy enough. All he had to do was to order the director of the Central

Bank to hand the money over to him. The director complied. Later the papers wondered what sort of legal basis, if any, existed for such a transaction.

The ethnic composition of Ecuador is as varied as her geography and history. If one keeps this in mind it is easy to understand why it has always been difficult to govern it and why it is politically and economically less stable than countries of comparable size on our old continent. To this day the inhabitants of Ecuador do not share a sense of national identity. The people of the Pacific coast, especially those the biggest city, Guayaquil, have very little in common with those who live in the Andes, in Quito, Otavalo or Cuenca. And, needless to say, life in the rainforest is totally different again. The cultural gap between the population of the countryside and that of the big cities is far greater in Ecuador than in any European state. The *blancos* of Ecuador feel much closer to their counterparts in Peru or Chile than to the *mestizos* or *indigenas* in their own country. The *indigenas* in the Andes, for example in the mountains surrounding Otavalo, lead a life very much apart from the rest of the population. They organise everything they need themselves. Their most important system of reference remains the tribal system. They hardly partake in the running of the country at all. The *indigenas* of the Andes have no connection whatsoever with the natives of the jungle.

There is one work of literature that attempted not only to capture the many different and often clashing traditions, ethnic groups and social classes of Ecuador but also to offer a vision of reconciliation between them. Juan Leon Mera in his novel *Cumandá,* first published in 1879, tells a story that comprises and connects all kinds of life in his country. I discovered this novel by accident. During my first visit to Ecuador, in the summer of 1995, I went to a bookshop in a street called Juan Leon Mera. There I came across the novel *Cumandá* and realised that the street was named after the author. I was interested in learning a little bit about Ecuadorian literature and eager to practice my Spanish and read the highly romantic and somewhat convoluted narrative.

Three years later I was travelling with Freddy through Ambato on the way to Chimborazo. To make conversation and because Freddy's office had been, when I first met him, located in the street named after Juan Leon Mera, I asked him if he knew the novel *Cumandá*. To my surprise he answered in the positive and told me that this novel is one of the key works of Ecuadorian literature, that it forms part of the curriculum in high schools and that in Ambato there was a fountain with a statue of Cumandá, the heroine of Juan Leon Mera's novel. A few minutes later we passed by that fountain and I got a glimpse of a sculpture representing the girl, who in the novel was an inhabitant of the rainforest and fell in love with the son of a white missionary. Both came to a sad but romantic end. A key work of the literature of Ecuador had fallen into my hands by sheer chance.

Ambato is the right place to host the statue of Cumandá. Firstly, Juan Leon Mera was born there. Secondly, it is situated on an important crossroads. Coming from Quito, which lies a few hours to the north, one turns to the left in order to descend to Baños and further towards the rainforest of El Oriente, and to the right if one wishes to climb Chimborazo or to go on further to Guayaquil on the Pacific coast. Ambato straddles the whole country in the same way that Juan Leon Mera's novel embraces the many facets of Ecuadorian life. *Cumandá* is more than a story of ill-fated love. Mera describes the lives of natives of the rainforest as well as of those in the Andean regions and of the *blancos*, who follow in the footsteps of the white *conquistadores*, and weaves them all together. Christians and pagans, whites and *indigenas* are connected by blood and common fate and by being part of the same fatherland, which Mera obviously loved very much and whose wild beauty he attempted to capture. The places where the drama unfolds are Riobamba, a small town some thirty kilometres to the South of Ambato, and the rainforest.

7.7 The girl from the jungle

Juan Leon Mera's novel is set around 1800. In the Amazonian rainforest at the meeting point of the Rio Palora and the Rio Pastaza live the pagan Jivaros and some tribes who have converted to Christianity. The chief of the Jivaros is Yahuarmaqui. The smallest of the Christian tribes consists of only one family: the old Tongana, his wife Pona, their sons and a daughter, Cumandá. Tongana is full of hatred against all white people.

Cumandá is secretly in love with a young white man with whom she has regular meetings. He is called Carlos and is the son of the missionary, Fray Domingo, whose full name is Juan Domingo Orozco and who is looking after the Christianised *Zaparos*. The missionary station is based in the village of Andoa.

Before he became a priest and a missionary, Juan Domingo Orozco had been a landowner south of Riobamba. One day, when he visited his oldest son Carlos who studied in a boarding school in Riobamba, a rebellion of the indigenous population against the white landowners broke out. Orozco's house was burnt down and his wife and four children were killed. The body of the youngest, Julia, was never found. The leader of the uprising was Tubon, a farmhand on Orozcos's estate, who had been treated very badly by his master. The rebellion was put down and Tubon was sentenced to death by hanging.

After these traumatic events Don Orozco entered a Dominican monastery. He finally accepted that he had been guilty of heartless and cruel treatment of the indigenous population. When he was offered the position of priest in the parish of Andoa he saw in this an opportunity to atone for his wrongdoings against the Indians. He allowed his son to go with him to Andoa.

Cumandá wants to become the wife of Carlos as soon as possible. However, as she has just been elected to be one of the *virgenes de la fiesta de las canoas*, the virgins of the festival of the canoes, she must keep away from her lover until the end of the fiesta. Carlos persuades Cumandá to let him take part in the festivities.

The sons of Tongana know about the secret meetings of their sister with Carlos. Tongana instigates them to kill Carlos but they must make it look like an accident, as murder would not be tolerated during the fiesta. Carlos is hit "by accident" with an oar and falls into the water. When Cumandá saves him, her feelings for Carlos become evident to all. It is apparent that she has broken her vow of chastity. Punishment for this crime is death. But as the festivities must not be desecrated by spilling blood, Yahuarmaqui postpones the execution till after the fiesta. Tongana has a better idea: he offers Cumandá as a wife to the chief, who accepts enthusiastically. To Tongana's disappointment, Yahuarmaqui is not prepared to kill Carlos because the alliance with the Christianised tribes is too important to him. Instead, he banishes him from the celebrations and orders him to return to Andoa the following morning.

During the night Cumandá escapes with Carlos. This probably saves their lives, as a few hours after their escape an enemy tribe attacks the unprepared Jibaros and their allies who are totally exhausted from the excesses of the fiesta. Luckily, one of the Christianised Indians hears the steps of the approaching attackers. He rings the alarm and the enemies are defeated in a bloody battle. Yahuarmaqui kills the chief of the enemy tribe in a dramatic duel. He thanks the Indian from Andoa who has raised the alarm by granting him the fulfilment of any wish he or his tribe may ask for.

The following day a messenger of the defeated tribe appears and offers Carlos and Cumandá, who were captured by his people, in exchange for the body of their killed chief. Yahuarmaqui is now prepared to execute Carlos, but the Andoan who has raised the alarm asks to pardon him. Carlos is sent back to Andoa and the wedding ceremony between Cumandá and Yahuarmaqui is carried out. The physical union is to take place in the following night. However, quite unexpectedly, the chief dies.

Custom demands that the favourite wife of the chief is to be killed and buried by the chief's side. No one doubts that Cumandá was his favourite. The funeral is to take place the following morning. In a solemn ceremony she will be drowned in aromatic waters. Cumandá's mother is one of the guards. She allows her daughter to slip away into the night. When Cumandá finds a boat tied up on the bank of the Palora River, she jumps in and lets it drift downstream towards Andoa.

In Andoa Fray Domingo alias Don Juan Domingo Orozco is awaiting the return of Carlos, who has rowed upstream with an Indian friend in order to look for Cumandá. He receives the news that a boat has drifted ashore with an unconscious woman in it. This is, of course, Cumandá. Then another boat appears with an emissary from the Jibaros. He tells Fray Domingo that Carlos has been captured. The demand is clear: give us Cumandá and we return Carlos to you. Should you refuse, we will kill your son. Before the reflection period granted to the missionary has expired, Cumandá hands herself over to the Jibaros.

After his return from captivity, Carlos persuades his father to organise a search party. Maybe there is still a way to save Cumandá. They find Tongana and Pona tied to a tree. This was in punishment for Pona having facilitated Cumandá's escape. Tongana is close to death. Pona now reveals his identity. Tongana is Tubon, the leader of the rebellion during which Orozco's family was wiped out. When he was hanged, the rope tore. He was thought to be dead and brought to the cemetery from where he escaped. Pona was his lover. She took mercy on Julia and saved her from Tubon's wrath. They brought her up as her own. So, Cumandá is the sister of Carlos!

Orozco realizes that this is the hour for repentance and forgiveness. He reveals his identity to the dying Tubon and asks him for forgiveness for the injustice he had inflicted on him. It is a highly emotional and operatic scene. At first Tubon is full of hatred and does not wish to contemplate forgiveness, but finally softens and forgives his enemy. Fray Orozco gives him absolution and Tubon can die in peace.

The Orozcos then move on in their search for Cumandá. They find the mummified bodies of Yahuarmaqui and Cumandá. She looks as if she were still alive. They bring her body back to Andoa and give her a Christian funeral. Soon after these sad events Carlos dies of a broken heart. His father has him buried beside Cumandá. On the day of Carlos' death Fray Domingo is called by his order to return to his monastery in Quito where he will continue his life of remorse and penance. The Zaparos remembered the story of the saintly missionary and of his lovable and unhappy children for a long time.

Thus ends the story of the love between Cumandá and Carlos, which turns out to be the love between siblings. But the book is about much more. It is a story about the political and social tensions between the repressed indigenous population and the white ruling class, about the life of the tribes in the forest, which at first sight seems to be like life in paradise but on closer analysis turns out to be plagued by similar evils which afflict the society of the white conquerors. It is a story about hatred, love and forgiveness, which encompasses all ethnic groups of the country. The novel offers a vision of a better future that has yet to happen.

7.8 The man from the jungle

After returning to Baños from our adventurous cycling excursion into the regions where Cumandá and Carlos lived and died so beautifully, we had dinner in my favourite restaurant, *El Marques*. It is situated beside the miracle-working waterfall that feeds the oldest of the thermal baths in the town. What made this restaurant particularly attractive for the visitor was that it provided good live music performances by multiple indigenous bands. There appeared to be an agreement among them never to stay too long in any one place so as to make room for others. *El Marques* attracted the biggest number of performers because of its ample interior with a special podium for the musicians. So, one was sure to be entertained musically at all times.

The restaurant was also popular among traders of the indigenous community who offered their chains, rings, bracelets and other costume jewellery to the tourist. Ursula bought a ring from one of those traders, and others followed her example. His selection was impressive enough and the prices were reasonable. But more interesting than what he had to sell was the story he told about himself. As he spoke quite good English, he had no difficulty in communicating with us.

His name was Juan and he was born in the rainforest. He grew up speaking only the language of his tribe. When he was seventeen years old both his parents died in a plane crash. We were wondering why inhabitants of the jungle were travelling in an aeroplane but we did not wish to interrupt him by asking irrelevant questions. An American woman took care of the orphaned teenager. She was a missionary and about forty years old. She cared so much for him that she made him her lover from which we deduced that she was a Protestant missionary. Not only did she teach him the techniques of love but she also taught him English. When she left the rainforest, she took Juan with her to Quito where he learned Spanish. Now, so he told us, and his voice dropped by a few notes and his eyes took on a melancholy expression, she is gone, she just left never to return. Nevertheless, he said, he was happy with his present life making his jewellery and selling it to tourists. We were very sympathetic with him and felt obliged to buy more of his articles. Perhaps, so we all hoped, he would someday meet another *gringa* whom he could teach some of the love techniques the missionary had instructed him in and further improve his English.

Here was a modern Cumandá story with swapped gender roles. Cumandá has become a young male and the missionary an American woman. The playground has become more global than in Juan Leon Mera's novel. But the essentials are still there; white civilisation meets tribal culture of La Amazonia. Because it was the late

20th century and the USA was involved the quality of the tale has become more like a Hollywood film with a happier ending.

San Francisco Church in Quito

Scrambling route to the summit of
Rucu Pichincha, November 2005

El Cotopaxi

The crater of Cotopaxi as seen from the summit

Market in Otavalo

Chapter 8: Chile 1997

8.1 Santiago de Chile

Ursula and I arrived in the capital of Chile on 9th December 1997. We planned to stay in the country until the middle of January 1998. As I was to attend a conference in early January in Concepción, we had planned our trip around this event. The conference was organised by ALEG, the *Asociación Latina Americana de Estudios Germanísticos* (The Latin American Association of German Studies). We looked forward to celebrating Christmas and New Year in the New World.

Whenever I travel to South America I like to stop over in Madrid. En route to Ecuador, I normally spend the night in the Spanish capital and fly out in the following morning. In this way I touch down in Quito at the perfect time of about 7:00 p.m. The evening in Madrid allows enough time to stroll to the Puerta del Sol and onward to the Plaza Major. There used to be a restaurant in the nearby Calle Mayor, called *El Naviego* where they served excellent lamb chops. This time, however, the schedule was different. We arrived in Madrid by 5:00 p.m. and the connecting flight to Santiago de Chile was due to take off at 1:00 a.m. This still gave us time to visit the Plaza Major and have a cosy meal in *El Naviego*. To our disappointment it was closed. So, we had a meal in another place that could not compete with our regular restaurant and then walked round the Plaza Major. The Plaza was done up in the fashion of an Austrian *Christkindlmarkt*. I bought a Russian looking fur hat that I still have.

It was around midday the following day when, after a short stopover in Buenos Aires, we landed in Santiago de Chile. The aeroplane dipped into dense fog and we saw nothing. Suddenly we got a glimpse of the Andes; naked gravelly ridges, hollows filled with dirty snow patches, some rugged peaks, stuck into a murky sky. It was a somewhat disappointing sight.

Señor N awaited us at the airport. He was the head of an organisation with the beautiful name *Amigos del Todo el Mundo*. These friends of the whole world helped travellers to find private accommodation all over Chile in what we call *Zimmer mit Frühstück* in German and B&B in English. Because this kind of accommodation was not common in Chile at that time (and may still not be) it was necessary to get in touch with the *amigos* before arrival. We were keen to stay at least some of our time in private accommodations because we felt that this would allow us to get to know some locals and see how they live. Is it not the dream of every true traveller to meet the real people and thus to really experience the real country?

We took the address of the *amigos* from the *Lonely Planet* and contacted señor N by fax, and here he was! He escorted us to his VW bus and drove us to the city. It was early summer and hot and humid. The grass was brown and sparse tufts of grass grew out of sandy soil. Señor N told us where we would be staying and gave us some information about our host family. He spoke very slowly so that I could understand every word. He was conscious of the fact that Chileans talk fast and swallow the ends of their words. Even people who have good Spanish, including native speakers, require some time to get used to the Chilean version of the Castilian idiom. I was grateful for his effort.

Our B&B was in the *Avenida Angustias,* some 15 minutes' walk from the city centre. M, our hostess, awaited us. She was around thirty, dark-haired and petite. Like her husband, J, whom we would meet later, she worked in a government office. She had taken a few hours off in order to welcome us and show us our room. As there was no lift, we had to haul our luggage up to the fourth floor. Lifts were not allowed, she informed us, because of the frequent earthquakes. Our room was tiny. The double bed took up most of it. It took us some time to arrange our suitcases and rucksacks till they finally fitted between the bed and the walls and still left some room for us to move about.

The plan was to spend seven days altogether in the Avenida Angustias, four days after our arrival and three days before our departure. Our hostess allowed us to leave part of our luggage behind so that we could travel light through the country. She did not expect any other guests. M and J enjoyed safe positions in the medium ranks of the civil service. They had no children and we got the feeling that they struggled somewhat to live a life style befitting their status. The approximately seventy square metre apartment, which they owned, consisted of one reception/living room and a small balcony, two bedrooms, of which we got the smaller, a kitchen with an adjoining utility room and two bathrooms. The rooms were very small. All the technical gadgets required by a modern household were there; a washing machine, TV, microwave, etc. Twice a week a woman came to clean the flat and to wash and iron the laundry. She was not exactly overworked. Most of her time she spent making tea and having endless telephone conversations with her friends.

Although jet lagged, we decided to walk into the city centre and have a look around. After changing dollars into Chilean pesos, we walked to the *Plaza de la Constitución* in front of the *La Moneda*, the presidential palace. Twenty-five years before, on 11th September 1973, the most horrendous scenes were played out there and shown on TV screens all over the world. Nobody who was alive then and old enough to grasp what was happening can ever forget them. Salvador Allende, the first democratically elected Marxist president of any South American country, was toppled and murdered by the rebellious Armed Forces led by general Augusto Pinochet. Pinochet enjoyed the support of the Nixon government and Henry Kissinger (who a year later received the Nobel Peace Prize – not for his shameful role in the uprising against Allende but for making peace with the Viet Cong by accepting American military defeat). I remember seeing the Chilean president on Austrian TV on that fateful day. Surrounded by a few of his supporters, who were willing to die with him, he stood on the balcony of the palace with a steel helmet on his head minutes before the Air Force began to bomb the palace. Troops stormed La Moneda and Allende was killed.

Immediately after the murder of the president and his closest comrades thousands of political opponents of the new military regime were detained in a stadium and most were never seen again. The human cost of that coup was horrendous. This was the first and original *Nine Eleven*! Allende's Marxist government had harmed nobody except the business interests of the United States. While the USA and her allies have made sure that the world would remember the second *Nine Eleven*, the crimes committed by Pinochet with the support of his Anglo-Saxon friends are largely forgotten. After Pinochet's brutal coup many Chileans suffered persecution, torture and illegal imprisonment for eight years. Yet, the rest of the world carried on as if nothing had happened. The attack on the Twin Towers, however, caused the angry North American giant to hit out indiscriminately and attack countries that had nothing whatsoever to do with the destruction of the symbols of American capitalism. The war on Iraq plunged the whole region into chaos from which it still has not recovered.

Well, here we were now in front of the meticulously renovated palace. In the warm sun people were strolling around in the park and sitting on benches. All was peaceful and nothing reminded of the horrors of the past, except, that there were more soldiers guarding the area than what might be considered "normal".

True, the country had returned to democratic rule, but what happened in 1973 was far from forgotten. Although democracy had been reinstated in 1990 it still appeared to be precarious. Augusto Pinochet had not gone away and had no intention of doing so. Now, in December 1997 he was still head of the Armed Forces and was finally asked to step down from this role. Giving up his leadership of the armed forces would have meant that he would lose his immunity from prosecution for crimes against humanity he committed during and after his *coup d'état*. Therefore, it was planned to make him a *senador vitalico*, a senator for life. As a *sena-*

dor vitalico he would enjoy immunity forever, he would become untouchable. The constitution allowed that democratically elected presidents of Chile could be given this honour after finishing their legal term. Salvador Allende should have been made *senador vitalico* had he not been murdered. Pinochet was not democratically elected. The media reported extensively about the controversy surrounding the ex-dictator. Every evening, in M's and J's flat, we saw him on TV. With his white hair, elegant white jacket and his friendly smile he did not look at all like a mass murderer, but more like a lovable uncle offering sweets to children.

The daily paper *El Sur* published a *resolución* drawn up by five members of the Chamber of Deputies that had been adopted by a majority of that chamber. They wanted to prevent Pinochet becoming a senator for life. The five instigators of the resolution were members of the ruling Christian Social Party (*Democracia Cristiana*). Their argumentation was decisive and clear. Here is what they had to say:

1. According to the High Command of the Armed Forces, General Pinochet will be made a *senador vitalico* within the next few weeks. This is a position which has been created in the constitution of 1980 for persons who have served the Republic for more than six years as president elected in democratic and free elections.

General Pinochet has not fulfilled this condition. He ousted the lawful president Dr Salvador Allende, by force and destroyed our democratic system for more than seventeen years.

General Pinochet held the office of president without ever having been elected by the people, and now he is set to become a senator for life in spite of this.

2. Nobody can pretend that under his government human rights had not been systematically violated. To this day, General Pinochet has not expressed any remorse for what he had done.

3. Amongst the countless Chileans who were affected by the repressive measures of the regime were the deputies who were holding office while the military putsch was happening. They were Carlos Lorca (Valdivia), Vicente Atencio (Arica) and Gastón Lobos

(Temuco). The first two were imprisoned and disappeared without a trace. The third one was executed.

This alone should be enough to make General Pinochet unsuitable for receiving the dignity of a *senador vitalicio*. It cannot be that somebody who headed a regime under which elected deputies were executed or made to disappear should be rewarded with a dignity that protects him from punishment.

4. The presence of General Pinochet in the Senate not only undermines the sovereignty of the people but also creates a climate, which is not conducive to the efforts of reconciling Chileans with each other and the restitution of the confidence of the civilian population in the military.

In addition to this, the presence of General Pinochet has a negative effect on the international reputation of our country.

5. For the above given reasons and especially in the interest of the efforts of reparation as well as because of the memory of the three murdered deputies we are of the opinion that the Chamber of Deputies has the moral duty to refuse the nomination of General Pinochet to senator for life.

The honourable Chamber of Deputies therefore adopts the following motion (*proyecto de acuerdo*) :

"The Honourable Chamber of Deputies is in agreement to make clear the refusal and rejection of making General Pinochet a senator for life. The Chamber regards his presence in the Senate as not helpful for the reconciliation of Chileans with each other and damaging the trust of the civilian population in the Armed Forces and harmful to the international reputation of Chile and especially of her Legislative."

As was to be expected, these clear and convincing arguments were brushed aside and Pinochet was made a senator for life in 1998. When he visited Britain in October 1998 he was detained because Spain had demanded his extradition. A Spanish judge wanted to charge him for the murder of Spanish citizens during his reign. After placing Pinochet under house arrest for sixteen months, the British government decided in March 2000 not to extradite him because of his alleged poor health and allowed him to return to Chile. Nevertheless, he lived for another six years. The

Chilean authorities tried several times to bring charges against him and put him under house arrest a few times. All these attempts failed and he finally died on 10th December 2006 at the age of 91.

From La Moneda we walked on and reached the Plaza de las Armas. There is a statue that remembers the sufferings of the indigenous population at the hands of the white *conquistadores*. The monument shows an Indian with his head placed at the side of his body. Everywhere in the world such monuments remembering past atrocities are only erected when it is too late to make amends.

The Plaza de las Armas also serves as a place where members of the public can speak freely. Religious sects use it to try to convert passers-by to their cause. Since the end of the military regime many Chileans have turned away from the Catholic Church that had so often betrayed the needs of the oppressed and the exploited by siding with the powers that be, no matter how evil they were. The vacuum the Catholic Church left behind was rapidly filled by an upsurge of all kinds of curious Protestant sects. One of the preachers we were watching appeared to suffer from serious convulsions. Was it his religion that had the effect of making the human body jump and twist in such an ugly way?

Our first impression of Santiago de Chile was somewhat disappointing. Maybe we expected to see historic buildings, like the splendid baroque churches in Quito. Because of the frequent earthquakes there is a dearth of historic architecture. People looked European. Most men wore suits and carried briefcases. Strolling around made us hungry. Pizza Huts and similar abominations dominated the scene. The type of restaurant we had in mind was nowhere to be seen. We asked a passer-by where the good or at least the better restaurants could be found. He was very polite and gave us his business card before he recommended the *Barrio Brasil*. From his card we learned that he was the director of a *pre-universitario* school. We followed his recommendation and had a good meal in the *Club Peruano*.

By 9:00 p.m. we were back in our B&B and met M's husband J. Ursula was tired and went to bed. I had a *pisco sour* with our hosts. Pisco is the Chilean national alcoholic spirit. It is made from residues of pressed grapes, in other words it is a Chilean grappa. *Pisco Sour* is a cocktail made of pisco, lemon, sugar and egg white. One prepares it like a whisky sour but with pisco instead and it tastes pleasantly refreshing. In most South American countries, the barmen know how to make good cocktails. They would not dream of offering premixed Margaritas and Caipirinhas, but they mix, shake or stir them right before your eyes. The food in some restaurants may be disappointing; the cocktails always make up for it. I told M and J about our first impressions of their city and cautiously mentioned the business about Pinochet. They called him Pinocchio and indeed this was the nickname the people had given him. In the following days we often saw "Pinocchio" sprayed on the walls of houses and underground stations.

The next morning, we took the underground to La Moneda. Approaching the station, we saw something resembling a big heap of rubbish. Getting nearer we realized that the heap was made of covers, rags and cloths on top of which two people were lying, a man and a woman, apparently in a deep sleep. It was half past ten in the morning.

The underground was most impressive. It was planned on a grand design and very clean. From La Moneda we walked alongside the river to *Cerro Santa Lucia*. This is a hill, in the middle of the city, covered by exotic trees. In the guidebook we had read that the summit offered good views. Walking up the hill, we came across a statue representing a wild Indian and a bit later the funeral chapel of Benjamin Vicuña McKenna, an important mid-19th century intellectual and journalist of Irish and Basque descent. The view from Cerro Santa Lucia was an anti-climax. Because Santiago was mostly covered in smog, the nearby Andes remained invisible. On the way down a few young people approached us, who were collecting money for their university. They told us that it had been privatised under Pinochet and was now in financial difficulties. We remembered that the previous day we were approached by another group of alleged students in the same manner with the same story. We were not sure what to make of it. Maybe it was a scam.

Heading from the underground station to our B&B we passed by what this morning we first thought to be a heap of rubbish. The woman was now sitting on the pavement and was eating something. A kettle was boiling while the man was gathering useful pieces of wood and plastics for their habitat. We saw those two every day during our stay in Santiago.

8.2 Viña del Mar on Election Day

On 11th December 1997 was Election Day. Offices and shops were closed. We decided to spend the day in the town of Viña del Mar. The bus ride takes an hour and a half and leads through a varied scenario of mountains and fields. Viña del Mar is a seaside town whose elegant suburbs are filled with grand villas from the turn of the 19th to the 20th century. The wealth of the town came from the saltpetre mines. When the Germans invented artificial fertiliser, the mines closed and the town declined. Today Viña del Mar is a tourist town, a popular weekend destination for the inhabitants of Santiago and many people have weekend- and summer-houses there.

On all public squares tables and chairs were set up. At each table sat a soldier in uniform and a civilian official who carried out the registration for election. The soldiers had the task of securing the orderly procedure of the democratic process. Watching this made us hungry. All restaurants were closed. We were told that during the elections the consumption of alcohol was strictly forbidden, and the only way of preventing restaurants from serving alcohol was to close them altogether. I thought of Ecuador where a similar law is applied less strictly. Restaurants are open and waiters discreetly place the bottle of wine or spirit under the table. Chile is more thorough. It is not for nothing that it has the reputation of being the Prussia of South America. Finally, we found a snack stand on a street corner where they sold *empanadas*. They could do so because they have no alcohol licence. Empanadas are pasta wraps filled with meat, fish or vegetables and are very popular. Ursula bought one filled with meat and I chose one with fruits of the sea. Both tasted horrible so we gave them to a stray dog. I was still hungry and I bought a *palmera* (pig's ear). I did not like it either and offered it to another dog. He turned his nose up at it.

After our unsuccessful attempts at finding somewhere to eat we decided to look at the wonderful houses. One of the most glorious villas of the Chilean Fin de Siècle had been converted into a museum and was now the *Casa de la Cultura*. It had belonged to a saltpetre baron and the Lonely Planet highly recommended a visit. The style of the house was that of a French chateau. In the park in front of the villa stood a sculpture by Rodin. To our disappointment it was closed. An elderly white-haired lady saw us standing around in a somewhat bewildered state and started talking to us. She told us about the fabulous wealth of the saltpetre barons and their ruination when the Germans invented artificial fertiliser. We asked her why the museum was closed today and she said it was because of the elections. In what ways could a visit to a museum pose a threat to the elections, I wanted to know. The friendly lady explained that the army was there to make sure that everything was done correctly and to protect the people when they cast their votes. Therefore, the soldiers have no time to guard museums and it was better to close them for the day. I asked if it really required the full force of the Armed Forces to protect the people during elections. Who are they protecting the people from? "From the terrorists" the friendly lady answered with a smile. Are there so many terrorists around, I could not resist to ask. "No, not today", she answered, "but in the past there were many. The country was then in a chaotic state because the Communists had taken over. The Army had to intervene to restore order..." She kept talking to us in that way for a while. She was really friendly and we finally said good-bye to each other most politely.

Back in Santiago we were really hungry. We ended up in a McDonald's. It was open because McDonald's never serves alcohol. We ordered hamburgers with chips. The hamburgers arrived without chips. We reordered chips and when they finally arrived, they were cold. We got cross and showed our disapproval in no uncertain manner. The manager came to our table, apologised profusely and offered us hamburgers without charge. This time they came with chips.

8.3 The Pan-American Highway; Christmas and New Year in Chile

The Pan-American Highway (*La Carrera Panamericana*) starts in Prudhoe Bay in Alaska and ends in Patagonia. It runs through Mexico and Central America, Colombia, Ecuador, Peru and Chile. Near Valparaiso north of Santiago de Chile it divides into two branches. Turning east into Argentina it leads via Buenos Aires to Ushuaia, in Patagonia where it ends. Continuing south from Valparaiso the highway brings the traveller to Puerto Montt and finally to Quellon at the southern tip of the peninsula of Chiloe.

When I was in high school a documentary film about the Pan-American Highway made a big impression on me. I thought that it must be one of the most exciting highways of the world leading the traveller through an incredible variety of peoples, cultures, landscapes and climates. The film described it aptly as one of the *Traumstaßen der Welt*, dream roads of the world. Ever since I dreamt of taking a year off to travel the whole way from Alaska to Patagonia. Like so many of my dreams, this one was never realised. However, I did travel parts of the Pan-American Highway several times, the first time in Ecuador in the year 1995. There it was a highway only in name. For the most part it was a rather bumpy affair full of *baches* (potholes), and crowded with the oddest looking, colourfully painted vehicles of more than doubtful roadworthiness.

When on 13th December 1997 we left Santiago by bus for Chillán in the South we were, once again, on this *Traumstraße*. The Pan-American Highway in Chile in 1997 was infinitely more civilised than in Ecuador. It was a real highway, wide and with a good surface. However, it was the only good road. As Chile is a very narrow country (between 80 and 160 km wide) but very long, the highway caters for most of the serious traffic. The trouble was, that as soon as one left it, one quickly ended up on dusty roads or on tracks covered with slippery gravel. It was a pleasure to travel in the superb buses of that country. They were extremely comfortable and safe. Each bus had two drivers who alternatively took over the wheel. Meals and refreshments were served. It was like flying first class. There was TV and sometimes everybody had to join a game of bingo whether one liked it or not.

We decided to visit Chillán because it was the birthplace of Bernardo O'Higgins. Ursula being Irish was keen to see the house where he was born. Bernardo was the illegitimate son of Sligo-born Ambrosio Bernardo O'Higgins and Isabel Riquelme. After emigrating to South America, Ambrosio became Captain General of Chile (1788 – 1796) and viceroy of Peru (1796 – 1801). His son Bernardo was instrumental in Chile's fight for independence from Spain and he is known in Chile as *El Libertator*. After a six and a half hour bus journey we arrived in Chillán and checked into *Hotel Libertator*. First on our agenda was to find the house where Bernardo O'Higgins was born. Only then we learned that it no longer existed. However, in its place was a statue of a military man on horseback and an impressive mural depicting scenes of the Battle of Roble. In this battle that took place on 17th October 1813, Chilean patriot forces took the city of Chillán from Spanish Royalists. Bernardo O'Higgins played a decisive role in achieving this victory.

The next day we continued south as far as Temuco, a rather uninteresting place that looks like many small towns anywhere in the United States. The following morning, we rented a car and drove to Chol-Chol, a Maipuche settlement some 30 km to the north. The road was appalling, the vegetation exquisite, and we saw oxen pulling ploughs and carts, something I had not seen since I was a child. On the way back we gave a lift to a young man. He told us that he was a psychologist, working with schools in the vicinity of Chol-Chol and Temuco, that his name was Mauricio and his *novia*, who was in her twenties, was seven months pregnant, and that they lived with his parents near our hotel. As we were always interested in getting ideas from locals as to where to eat well, we asked him for his advice. He recommended a restaurant that served excellent *platos tipicos* of Chile, such as *empanadas* and *humitas*. We went there in the evening full of expectations, but they had neither *empanadas* nor *humitas*.

Two days later we drove to the *refugio* at the foot of the over three thousand metre high *Volcán Llaima*. There was no chance of us climbing that mountain as it was snow covered and we had no proper equipment, but we thought that we might be able to do a short walk. In the village of Vilcun we stopped at a tourist office to get information about walking options. While the lady in the office tried to persuade us not to go back to Temuco tonight but to stay longer in the area, a German man appeared and told us that he could rent us a *cabaña* (holiday house), complete with sauna, mountain bikes and horse-riding options. As his prices were a bit stiff, we said that we would think about it, but right now we were looking for advice how hike on Llaima without getting lost. He suggested an easy route and we agreed to look at his cabañas on the way back.

Following his advice we drove up to the *refugio* and walked about an hour and a half over a snowfield towards the volcano alongside pylons. The spectacular views were somewhat spoiled by the ski lifts that were lying idle as it was early summer. We were wondering what had brought our German friend, whom we estimated to be in his mid-forties, to Chile. He had told us that he came in 1982 and that he had only once been back to Germany. Pinochet's rule ended in 1990. We had no opportunity to ask him because by the time we returned from our hike it was too late to stop in Vilcun to see his cabañas. Back in Temuco we had no desire to eat again in the restaurant where we got neither *empanadas* nor *humitas* the previous night, but decided to try the local *Club Aleman* (German Club).

In the middle of the 19th century Southern Chile had a considerable influx of German and Austrian immigrants, whose influence can be seen in the architecture of the houses and in the existence of German Clubs in most of the bigger towns. Each *Club Aleman* has a restaurant that looks like a traditional *Gasthaus* with a *Schank* (a bar), and a *Stammtisch* (a table for regular customers). The restaurant of the Club in Temuco turned out to be of a high standard. At the *Schank* we ordered a *picso sour* each. The recipe includes a small quantity of egg white to be added to the mix. Instead of splitting the egg in two and separating the yoke and the egg white, the barman punched a little hole in the top end of the egg and when he turned it upside down the egg white came out leaving the yoke behind. Dinner consisted of *Kassler Rippchen mit Sauerkraut und Bratkartoffeln* accompanied by *Beck's Bier*. It made us feel really good.

The next day, as we drove in our rented car from Temuco towards Pucon, in the Chilean Lake District we passed by the town of Villarica. Half way between Villarica and Pucón, near the shores of *Lago Villarica* we came across a sign advertising *cabañas* for rent. We now knew what a cabaña was and followed the sign. In the middle of a small forest we found a settlement of lovely houses grouped round a swimming pool. As it was off-season we rented a cabaña for the ridiculous price of twelve dollars a day. It was comfortable and well equipped and we decided to stay for Christmas and a few days beyond. The lake was only a few hundred metres away, and a fifteen minute drive would take us to the town of Pucon. There were plenty of opportunities for excursions by car and on foot.

On the evening of our arrival, we were lying in deck chairs by the pool drinking picso sours and smoking small Montecristo cigars. The owner of the holiday homes had two poodles, both bitches. Bini was the mother and Pancha the daughter. They were friendly dogs, and Pancha kept nudging me to throw stones for her to catch. A stray cat came into our house and made herself at home. Every day she got more attached to us as Ursula kept feeding her *Whiskas*. A hen and a rooster spent the night in a tree outside our bedroom. Around sunset we watched them settling onto a branch, it was always the same one, to sleep beside each other. We did not need an alarm clock as every morning the crowing rooster woke us up at 6:00 a.m. on the dot.

The following morning we drove to nearby *Lago Caburga* and hired a rowing boat. From the middle of the lake we enjoyed splendid views of Volcán Villarica, the summit of which was 2,847 m high and covered in snow. Ever so often the crater emitted a cloud of smoke. On Friday, 19th December, we drove to the *Huerquehe National Park*, a short distance east of Pucon, and managed to walk five and a half hours, covering a distance of ten kilometres and climbing eight hundred metres. We followed an easy path, through lush forests passing by a number of mountain lakes: *Lago Tinquilco, Lago Chico, Lago Verde* and *Lago El Toro*. The snow-capped Volcán Villarica was in sight the whole time. Driving back to our cabaña we gave a lift to a young woman from the Netherlands. She was travelling alone for five weeks through Chile and Argentina and had climbed Volcán Villarica a few days earlier.

Inspired by that courageous women I decided to climb Villarica at the earliest opportunity. We stopped in Pucon and I booked a guided tour to the summit for the following day. I tried on boots, crampons and chose an ice axe. From what she saw, Ursula concluded that this mountain was more than just a stroll and opted for staying by the pool.

Back in our cabaña a second cat joined us. This one was a tom, and even more relaxed in the house than the female cat, which, as we now noticed, was pregnant.

I successfully climbed Volcán Villarica. The guides divided us into two bigger groups of between fifteen and twenty people each and a smaller party of eight. The bigger groups were to take a chairlift to a certain point and walk from there, the smaller party would walk all the way. I went with the smaller party. Apart from myself there were two Israelis, a Swiss couple, a Swedish-Chilean couple and a young American man who had been to Ecuador and climbed Cotopaxi. The ascent was easier than I had expected. After a misty start the sun came out and we had a glorious day. An hour before reaching the top we could smell the sulphur of the volcano and the ground got noticeably warmer. The top of the mountain consisted of an enormous crater whose toxic fumes almost knocked one out. Some climbers had gas masks that made them look like soldiers from the trenches of World War I. The most spectacular sight was that of the 3,800 m high *Volcán Lanín* fifty kilometres away in Argentina. At 4:30 p.m. we were all back in Pucon.

I returned to our cabaña and joined Ursula by the pool. Before going to sleep we said good night to the rooster and the hen on their branch. The few days before Christmas we spent the time visiting the beaches of lakes Villarica and Caburga, river rafting and driving to the Argentinian border. On one of our outings we met two young women who we first took for Chileans but turned out to be Israelis. They were travelling through South America for five months. I could not help envying them. Another time near the Argentinian border we noticed a very formally dressed man walking alone on the dusty road in the heat of midday. He asked us for a lift to the next village which we gladly gave him. He was a Jehovah Witness and, like all the evangelists of different persuasions, incredibly dedicated to his mission.

We had noticed that in Chile evangelist movements were booming. The halls where they congregated tended to be full of enthusiastic people clapping their hands and singing their hearts out. By contrast, the Catholic churches were sadly empty. Most likely this was one of the consequences of the Pinochet dictatorship. The people turned away from a Church that had sided with the brutal regime. This was, of course, not the first time the Catholic Church had supported the powers to be against those in need of Christian kindness. From the late 18th century onward, the Church everywhere had backed various *Ancien Regimes* in their efforts to suppress any movements that were directed against them. By doing this, the Church lost the support of the working classes to the Socialist and Communist movements in the late 19th and the first half of the 20th centuries. Rome learned nothing from her mistakes and continued to back the wrong horse: the fascists, Franco, the Nazis and the atrocious dictatorships in South and Central America.

That evening we noticed that our rooster was sitting alone on his branch. When asked, our hostess told us that the hen had been sacrificed for the pot. We felt really sorry for our rooster who was now a widower.

On 24th December our little settlement of cabañas suddenly was filled with guests. Since it was Christmas Eve, the trees of our forest were lit up with electric candles. It was all very festive, but because of the summer like temperatures it did not really feel like Christmas. Before sitting down to Christmas dinner we drank champagne by the pool with an international family. The man was Swedish, his wife Finnish and they lived in Finland. With them were their two daughters, one of whom had been adopted in Chile.

On 28th December we left our pleasant cabaña, Bini and Pancha, the widowed rooster, the stray tom and the pregnant cat, for Puerto Montt, a five hours drive away. The weather had turned bad. It was now raining constantly. Puerto Montt is known for its rainy climate. I do not remember much of that town except that everything was dripping wet. In the restaurant where we took our evening meal, we met two American ladies who were travelling with a British walking club. Tomorrow, they told us, they were embarking on a freight ship to Puerto Natales in Patagonia, which sounded very exciting to us.

Another option of travelling towards Patagonia is driving the *Carretera Austral* from Puerto Montt 1,240 km to Villa O'Higgins. This is about half way down to the Southern tip of the continent. Most people take the far better road to Patagonia that runs through

Argentina. The *Carretera Austral* (Southern Highway) was built during the dictatorship of Augusto Pinochet. Much of it was a dirt road, the petrol pumps were scarce and one was, therefore, advised to bring a few canisters of petrol or diesel in the four-wheel drive. From what I have read, the Carretera Austral must be one of the most spectacular drives in the world. One passes by glaciers and fjords and the journey involves three crossings by car ferry of between forty-five minutes and five hours. I regret that this remains another of my unrealised dreams. At my age I will most likely have to postpone it to my next life.

The following day, however, we ventured some fifty kilometres into the Carretera Austral, just to see what it was like. We very quickly realised that our rented car could not survive the rough surface and the potholes. Back in Puerto Montt we went for dinner in the local *Club Aleman* and once again we were not disappointed. The restaurant was full of people and festively decorated with garlands and lanterns. A TV crew was making a programme about the New Year celebrations in Puerto Montt. We all had to behave as if we were celebrating the arrival of the New Year. The result of their work would be broadcast on 31st December. Ursula and I had the honour of being briefly interviewed ("Where are you from? How do you like Chile?") We never saw the programme. The meal was more than satisfying. After two potent Margaritas we had an enormous fish platter and a bottle of wine. It was all great fun and we were looking forward to celebrate the arrival of 1998 in great style. This was to happen in two days' time in Castro on the island of Chiloe.

We left Puerto Montt on 30th December in glorious weather and crossed by ferry to the island of Chiloe. Our hotel in Castro was pleasant. There were very few guests. On the last day of 1997 we drove to Quellón in the South of the island. It is there that the Chilean variant of the Pan-American Highway ends. Standing at the tip of the island and looking south we got a tempting glimpse of some snow-covered mountains alongside the Carretera Austral.

In the evening we dressed for a festive New Year's dinner and walked down to the restaurant of our hotel. Everything was in darkness and nobody was around. After a while the owner appeared and informed us that the hotel kitchen was closed because of the holiday. When she saw the disappointment in our faces, she recommended a restaurant called *Palafito* and kindly offered to drive us there. The restaurant was empty and the waiter appeared to have had a few drinks too many. When we asked him what kind of *cocteles* he could offer he did not seem to know what a *coctel* was. However, he was familiar with the word *aperitivo*. I forgot what *aperitivo* we had, if any, but I remember the crab we ordered. Anytime I have had crab in Spain it was served cold and tasted delicious. In *Palafito* the crabs were lukewarm and tasteless. The whole thing was an anti-climax.

After having had enough of the disappointment we asked for a taxi back to the hotel. There was none to be had, so we staggered back in the dark. Ursula took off her shoes because she did not want to ruin them on the uneven surface. Back in our room we turned on the TV and watched the celebratory fireworks in Valparaiso. They looked impressive. It was obvious that we were in the wrong place. We opened a bottle of warm Coca Cola, mixed it with Pisco and welcomed the New Year.

Lago Caburga and the Villarica Volcano

Chapter 9: Venezuela 2000

9.1 First impressions of Caracas

> Caracas in 1975 was happy and chaotic, one of the world's most expensive cities. New buildings and broad highways were springing up everywhere and money was being squandered on a surfeit of luxuries; there were bars, banks, restaurants, and hotels for love nests on every corner, and the streets were permanently clogged by the thousands of late-model automobiles that could not move in the pandemonium of the traffic. No one respected traffic lights, but they would stop dead on the freeway to let some distracted pedestrian cross. Money seemed to grow on trees; thick wads of bills changed hands with such speed that there was no time to count them (…) (Isabel Allende, *Paula*).

This was the impression the city of Caracas made on Isabel Allende when she arrived there in 1975, after having fled her own country from Pinochet's dictatorship. It was then the height of the oil boom and there seemed to be no end in sight to many years of assured economic growth. A rosy future appeared to lie ahead for everybody.

However, the bonanza did not last forever. In February 2002 Venezuela was in deep crisis. The economy was in ruins and corruption was as rampant as ever, the poor were getting poorer by the day, and the government of the populist ruler Hugo Chavez came under heavy fire from the opposition. During my short visit to Caracas in October 2000 I sometimes turned on the TV in my hotel room and saw the *jefe del estado* prancing about in a general's uniform covered with medals, in simple combat dress or in elegant attire, whatever was best suited to the occasion. It did not seem to matter *what* he was doing; the important thing was to be seen: visiting a mine, boosting the moral of troops stationed in the jungle, receiving a foreign statesman, delivering a harsh speech against the trade unions etc. He was omnipresent and most of the ordinary people I talked to seemed to support him. They believed him to be efficient, well-intentioned, caring genuinely for the poor, and determined to once and for all end the endemic corruption that had plagued the country for so long. In 2002 the tide began to turn against him. A coup was attempted but failed and he ruled on until he died of cancer in 2013.

Now, as I am writing this in 2021, Venezuela has finally plunged into complete chaos. This is not only very sad, but difficult to understand. With her mineral riches and fantastic potential for tourism, Venezuela's economy should be like that of Norway or even better. Nicolás Maduro, the disputed president, blames the United States for the economic and political crisis of his country. Guilty as the USA may be for many things wrong in South America, it seems that the failure of Venezuela is largely homemade.

I arrived in Caracas on the evening of Monday, 2nd October 2000. I was there to attend a conference of ALEG, the *Asociación Latinoamericano de Estudios Germanisticos*. Stepping out of the Air France plane the warm and humid air embraced me. As it was close to sunset, the temperature had dropped to a pleasant 28° C. I had booked my hotel over the Internet and was supposed to get a *traslado aeropuerto – hotel*. After waiting and wandering about for some twenty minutes it became obvious that there was no *traslado*. Then I caught sight of a small group in which someone held up a plaque with ALEG written on it. I rejoiced and introduced myself. They were, in fact, waiting for some members of the conference who had not disembarked from the plane on which they were supposed to arrive. They knew nothing about me, but this was not surprising, as I had arranged my own *traslado* via the local agency. One of the women in the group was a lecturer in German in the Universidad Central. She kindly offered to give me a lift to the Hotel Avila where I was (hopefully) booked in. In this way I got my first introduction to the traffic chaos.

Isabel Allende had not exaggerated. Never before or since have I experienced such chaos on the roads. Memories of Naples, where I had been as a hitchhiker in the late sixties came back to me. This, however, was different. It was a higher category of chaos. What

Allende said was true; nobody gave a hoot about traffic lights nor speed limits nor one-way systems. Cars made U turns in the most impossible situations. Needless to say, we were overtaken on either side and my driver in turn overtook wherever the opportunity offered itself. The utterly amazing thing was that in spite of this chaos, the traffic kept moving. If a vehicle made a U turn and moved against the tide, nobody expressed irritable feelings by shouting or blowing the horn. If the horn was blown it was rather meant as a warning as if to say: "Take care I am going to make a U turn", or "If you insist on making a U turn here, please make sure not to bump into my car, thank you." As everybody offended against the norms it seems to have become the norm to do so. Knowing this, everybody acted accordingly. For my whole stay I could not help admiring this orderly and cheerful chaos again and again.

Of course, it is not only the traffic that is chaotic. Life in general is chaotic in Venezuela. Rules and regulations, without which Europeans and North Americans seem unable or unwilling to live, do not have much value there. They exist on paper, but that is where they remain. Who knows, perhaps the climate has something to do with it. As I was looking in amazement at what was happening around us, I remembered a tape I had once listened to in the Instituto Cervantes in Dublin. A woman from Venezuela talked about the attitudes towards life in her country. She pointed out that, because there were no seasons in Venezuela, plants never die. Part of a plant dies, but new parts replace the dead bits so that the plant lives on more or less indefinitely. This had, so the speaker explained, a profound influence on the attitude of her compatriots towards time. Since there are no seasons and no obvious end to life, at least not to the life of plants, Venezuelans do not share the obsession of Europeans and North Americans with time and, consequently, with order. When I listened to that tape many years ago, I found the thesis expressed there interesting but took it to be no more than a stimulating academic point. Now I began to dawn on me that it might be actually true

9.2 Dangers

Caracas has a reputation for being a dangerous city. The crime rate is very high, and if one goes for a stroll in any of the central districts one risks being robbed or even killed. All the people living in Caracas kept warning us visitors to be very careful. As we left the motorway and struggled through the dense traffic of the inner city, I noticed that hardly any pedestrians could be seen on the pavements. It was dark and it was a balmy evening. Yet as we drove by the Hilton Hotel and the Plaza Venezuela, I could count the pedestrians on one hand. Occasionally a group of young people stood on a street corner. Perhaps they were waiting for some naïve *gringo,* with an expensive camera round his neck and his pockets full of dollars to pounce upon. Once I was warned about the dangers of Caracas I could not help spotting danger signs all around me.

I thought of Madrid, my usual stop over point en route to South America. In the summer the streets of the Spanish capital are crowded with pedestrians. The climate lends itself to roaming the streets at night and everybody is outdoors. In Caracas the climatic conditions are similar, in fact even better. Madrid has warm weather between May and September. Caracas is warm all the time. The capital of Venezuela could be the world capital of pedestrians. Instead, it is, like Los Angeles, a metropolis of car drivers. Not only did I not see pedestrians, there were no street cafes either. Perhaps it is not only dangerous to walk on the pavements but also to sit outside a café.

The approach to the Hotel Avila was an impressive avenue lined with palm trees. We had to pass a gate guarded by armed security. Only the previous day an international conference of oil producing countries (OPEC) had ended and many participants were still in town, some of them were staying in this hotel. At the reception I was pleased to be told that my room was reserved. I complained about not being picked up from the airport as arranged and the receptionist promised to look into the matter. I heard no more of it.

In the following days I took the warnings against street robbers to heart and hardly dared to wander around. To get from the hotel to the conference centre was a five-minute walk. To go anywhere further I took a taxi. This was fine until scary stories about taxis in Caracas began to circulate. One of my colleagues, G, told me what had happened to an Argentinian professor a year before. Well, this poor man, let us call him Alfredo, arrived in Caracas shortly after nightfall. He took the first taxi available. Because it was dark, he could not take a closer look at it. He told the driver the name of the hotel and off they went. After a few minutes the driver stopped and took in two more passengers. Alfredo thought this to be a bit strange, but, perhaps, this was the custom in Caracas. He was mistaken. The two new passengers were robbers, who worked with the driver, who was not a bona fide taxi driver, but a robber posing as a taxi driver, apparently a common occurrence in Caracas. The two new 'passengers' threatened Alfredo with a gun, took his credit card and asked him for the PIN number. If he did not tell the number, they informed him politely but firmly, they would have no choice but to shoot him. What could the poor man do but to give them the PIN number? The held him prisoner until they had spent all his credit.

I was unsure as to whether or not to believe G. I knew her to be a person who experienced horrific misadventures wherever she went, and her friends also seemed to have alarming adventures when travelling. I decided to keep away from her.

9.3 Hiking on El Avila

Wherever I am I like to climb a mountain if there is one nearby. Caracas is beautifully situated. It lies about 1,000 m above sea level. To the north is *El Avila,* a range of mountains that separates Caracas from the sea. It has various peaks, the highest of which, *Pico Naiguatá,* is 2,765 m high. *El Avila* is a National Park with well-maintained trails. It offers a wide choice of hikes. If one carries a tent one can walk the whole range of mountains. My Venezuelan colleagues assured me that I needed not to worry about robbers. Many people walk the paths and muggers seem to find it more profitable to hang about busy street corners in the centre of the city. G had expressed an interest in going for a hike. Because of her association with unlucky events and persons I thought it wiser to go on my own.

One of the treks started right behind the hotel. There were many people of all ages, single, in pairs and in groups heading in the direction of the mountains. Many of them were women who walked alone. It must be safe. I asked two young men if this was *el camino hasta El Avila*. They asked where I wished to go. I had no idea. I did not even have a map. All I wanted was to reach a good viewpoint. They said they were going to *Lagunazo* and invited me to join them. I accepted enthusiastically. It was a good opportunity to meet inhabitants of Caracas and get to know the surroundings of the city under local guidance.

Initially we walked on a narrow and small road that was paved with cobblestones and used by the occasional *camioneta* (pickup truck). My friends waved one down and all three of us jumped on and thus gained height very quickly. When we came to a point where the road was blocked by a broken down car we got off and continued on foot. Soon the paved road came to an end. We now followed a winding path moving through different climatic zones. At first, we walked through a type of savannah and then through forests whose character has, over the years, been changed by human interference. We saw eucalyptus trees that were imported at the beginning of the 20th century. Between 1,000 and 2,000 m we moved through cloud forest, and finally reached the plateau that runs from East to West and contains various peaks.

Caracas was behind us and the sea was in front. Because of the heavy mist we could see neither. What we did see, however, was a skyscraper, so tall that the top disappeared in the thick clouds. It was the recently built Hotel Humboldt, not yet open to the public. The opening was supposed to happen once the cable car was completed. On the way up we had come across various building sites of this proposed cable car. It all looked like a very long way from being completed. There was once a cable car that brought visitors to a viewing point a few hundred metres above the city. When the German company in charge left, it fell into disuse. For the past ten years various governments had planned to revive and extend the cable car, so far without success. I had the feeling that by the time the *teleférico* would be completed the Hotel Humboldt may well have fallen into ruins.

A German novel, *Der Schlangenbaum*, by Uwe Timm came to my mind. It is set in an unnamed South American country. The protagonist, a German engineer, has to make his way on roads which suddenly end somewhere in the jungle, and at one stage he has to get across a river whose bridge ends half way, in mid-air and shows no sign of ever been completed. The country is filled with white elephants, started by various dictators who have long been replaced by others who, in turn, started their own projects, which inevitably suffered the same fate of incompletion as the previous ones.

From the Hotel Humboldt we moved along in an easterly direction. The path now was interrupted by deep gorges, which had been created by the torrential rains of December 1999. We had to climb down into these gorges and scramble out of them on the other side and look for the continuation of the path. There was mud underfoot and it was easy to imagine how quickly the path must become impassable once rain falls. After a further one and a half hours we finally reached *Lagunazo*. This is an area with tundra-like vegetation. A subterranean lake provides it with many springs. It was now five o'clock in the afternoon and we were some 2,200 m above sea level. The mist had lifted and we could see the coast. As it would be dark by seven o'clock my friends decided not to go back the way we came but to descend into the village of Galipán on the north side of the mountain.

Descending into Galipán we had to cross more gorges created by the rains of the previous year. We saw houses perched precariously close to the abyss. They looked as if they had narrowly escaped being washed away completely. Some were badly built and many had windows without glass. Others were surrounded by splendid gardens full of exotic flowers.

Galipán is connected to Caracas by a road that is passable by four-wheel drives only. There was a small fair going on. Children were riding ponies, music was blaring from loudspeakers, there were stalls offering refreshments and a grocery. We sat down and had something to eat and to drink. I wanted a beer but no alcohol was available. We managed to get a lift on one of the many *camionetas* back to Caracas. My friends insisted on walking me back to the hotel, as they were concerned for my safety.

I was very impressed by the kindness of these young Venezuelans. The two lads were the first locals I had met and they were extremely friendly and easy-going. During the rest of my stay, I had a few more good experiences. In spite of everything I had been told by my colleagues at the conference, I only met friendly people in Caracas.

Two days later Germany celebrated the tenth anniversary of the fall of the Berlin wall and the German Embassy in Caracas invited all the participants of ALEG to a reception. So, there was something to look forward to for the evening. I had become a bit tired of going to all the lectures at the conference. There comes a point when I can take no more of academia and that had been reached by then. I decided to do another hike up *El Avila* by a different route. As my first experience had been so positive, I concluded that even being in the company of my catastrophic friend G would not pose an undue danger and asked her to come along.

9.4 Taxis, robbers and Siemens-girls

A taxi type vehicle was waiting for business in front of the Hotel Avila most of the time. As G and I were about to get in, G suddenly noticed that it displayed no official taxi sign. She had been warned by her Argentinian friend to make sure to use only officially registered taxis. So, she said to the driver: *usted no es un taxi oficial*. He confirmed that his car was not a taxi but that it belonged to the hotel and that he drove clients of the hotel to wherever they wanted. As we had seen him and his car many times during the past days, we trusted him and got into his car. He dropped us off at our starting point and assured us that it would be easy to get a taxi to bring us back.

Our hike was pleasant and safe. We arrived back at our starting point at three o'clock in the afternoon, soon enough to return to the hotel, have a rest and get ready to celebrate the fall of the wall. All we needed now was a taxi. The streets were deserted. It was hot and everybody seemed to be enjoying a siesta. We sat down on the pavement and waited for a taxi. None appeared. After some time, we noticed two men standing in front of a parked car. They had the bonnet opened and were peering at the engine. We asked them where we would find a taxi rank and they told us that the best thing to do was to wait. Sooner or later a taxi was bound to turn up. After we had been waiting another twenty minutes, the man with whom we had spoken approached us and offered to drive us to the nearest taxi rank. We hesitated only briefly before accepting with relief. Once in his car (his friend had disappeared) he asked us where we were staying. When we told him it was the Hotel Avila he said he would drive us there. We protested weakly but were really delighted to get back to base quickly.

Our conversation with the driver soon turned to the topic of security and he warned us of the dangers of Caracas. Especially, he said, we ought to be extremely weary of motorists offering us lifts. Many would do so with the intention of robbing the trusting tourist. He assured us that he was, of course, no robber. However, he was trying to impress on us to be extremely careful. For a moment I feared that we might have fallen into the hands of a robber, who was trying to gain our confidence by warning us against robbers. Perhaps I had made a mistake getting into a car together with G the catastrophist. After listening to his well-intentioned advice for a few minutes we suddenly were in front of our hotel. Our driver opened the car door for us and wished us a pleasant stay. He was no robber but another of the many friendly inhabitants of Caracas.

A few days later a German professor told me of an adventure he had a few years previously. He was leaving a party at three o'clock in the morning and looked for a taxi. The streets were empty. However, on a street corner he noticed a parked car with the bonnet opened. A man was bending over it and, to all appearances, carrying out some repair. The car was a taxi. So our man, let us call him Peter, approached the driver and asked him for a lift to his hotel. The driver agreed, closed the bonnet, and Peter sat in the car. The hotel was a well-known hotel in a well-known area. However, it quickly became obvious that the driver was no taxi driver. He did not appear to be from Caracas either as he did not have a clue where he was going. Peter directed him as best as he could and after driving all over the city, getting lost many times, doing the usual U turns on highways and driving against many one-way streets, they reached the hotel. Peter got out of the taxi and he had hardly closed the door when the driver pulled off with screeching tyres and disappeared in a cloud of dust. Peter came to the conclusion that his driver had been a stranger to Caracas who had just been in the process of stealing the taxi when he was asked for a lift. In order not to be caught, the thief must have thought it was wise to pretend to be a *taxista* and to perform this role as best he could. Well, Peter got to his hotel, what more did he want?

The German ambassador's reception took place in the *Hotel Gran Meliá Caracas*, which was the biggest and most expensive hotel in the city. Most of the big shots of the OPEC countries had stayed there. The reception room was on the first floor and enormous. Everybody who was anybody in the country was here, including the sizable German community. Entering the room, we all shook hands with the ambassador and his wife. There were also quite a few girls, who were specially chosen for their looks, standing around the entrance. They were absolutely stunning. None was more than twenty years old. They had gorgeous black hair, dark eyes, immaculate skin and perfect proportions. They were dressed in very short miniskirts. Some seemed to be uncomfortable in them as they kept pulling the skirts down (which did not make them any longer). The blouses worn by the girls were printed with names of well know German firms. There was a SIEMENS girl, a BASF girl, a BAYER girl and so on.

I was not quite sure what to make of this, until a colleague pointed to the invitation card. On the card it said: *La Embajada agradece a las empresas que patrocinan el evento* (The Embassy thanks the firms which sponsor the event). The firms were: Deutsche Bank, Siemens, Merck, Bayer, Beck's, D'Ambrosio Hermanos, Waveca, Dresdner Bank Lateinamerika AG y Dresdner Bank AG, Ferrostaal, DSD, Veba Oel, Mont Blanc, Thyssen Rheinstahl Technik, Industrial Esco S.A., Boehringer Ingelheim Pharmaton, Verimpex C.A., Lufthansa, BASF, Aventis, Mannesmann, Mercedes Benz, Preussag Energie. The beautiful local girls served as live posters for the firms, which sponsored the event thus turning the celebration into an advertisement. It was a rather embarrassing affair. When we left the party we were told that we could take free gifts from the stands of the various firms. Some of my friends walked away with SIEMENS T Shirts or Lufthansa bags. I would have liked a real Mercedes Benz, but as none was available.

Chapter 10: Brazil 2003 and 2004

10.1 Land of the future

From 25th September to 5th October 2003, I was lucky to once again attend a conference of ALEG, the Latin American Association of German Studies. This time it took place in Brazil where I had never been before. What particularly attracted me was the fact that this was a "wandering conference": At first, we were to spend a few days in Sao Paolo, then move on to Paraty and Petropolis and finally to Rio de Janeiro.

Now, most of us have some kind of notion about Rio de Janeiro. I knew very little about Sao Paolo and I had never heard of Paraty, the charming 17th century colonial town on the coast. The only thing I knew about Petropolis was that the Austrian writer Stefan Zweig and his second wife Charlotte Altmann had committed suicide there and that one could visit their grave. My guidebook informed me that the villa where the Zweigs had lived still existed, but that it was privately owned and not open to visitors.

Many years ago, I had read quite a lot of Zweig's work and I had been particularly impressed by his biographies of Marie Antoinette, Fouché and Magellan. When the Nazis took over Austria and Europe he and his wife fled to England, New York and South America. They ended up in Brazil, a country about which Zweig was very enthusiastic. In his book *Brasilien. Ein Land der Zukunft* (Brazil, Land of the Future), published in 1941, he describes Brazil as a place where people of different ethnic and cultural background, race and colour had learned to live together in harmony. He did not commit suicide because he found Brazil a hard place to live. He did so because he thought that Europe was doomed forever, something he could not bear: "I think it better to conclude in good time and in erect bearing a life in which intellectual labour meant the purest joy and personal freedom the highest good on Earth." In 2016 Maria Schrader's marvellous Film *Vor der Morgenröte* with Josef Hader in the role of Stefan Zweig was released. It follows Zweig's last years in New York and South America and ends with his and Charlotte's suicide in Petropolis.

Petropolis is located high in the mountains away from the heat of the coast. Because of its cooler climate it was the perfect summer retreat for the rich of Rio de Janeiro, which until 1960 was the capital of Brazil. There are some fabulous villas that were built for the so-called coffee barons, and the Emperor of Brazil had his summer palace there. In the 20th century some of the presidents of the country used the palace as their summer residence.

You may ask why and when there was an Emperor of Brazil. It has to do with Brazil gaining independence from Portugal. This is how it happened: In 1808 the Portuguese king John VI was driven out of his country by Napoleon. He fled to Brazil, which was a Portuguese colony. On 16th December 1815 he made Brazil a kingdom. In 1821 he returned to Portugal and handed over the rule of the new kingdom to his son, who became Pedro I of Brazil. On 7th December 1822 Pedro declared independence from Portugal. He was appointed emperor of Brazil on 12th October and crowned on 1st December of the same year. A short war followed after which Portugal recognised Brazil's independence in the Treaty of Rio de Janeiro of 1825. When king John VI of Portugal died, Pedro was invited to succeed him on the throne. However, he forfeited his right and remained in Brazil. Maria II became queen of Portugal. In 1831 the Brazilian parliament forced the resignation of Pedro I in favour of his son, Pedro II who was still a minor. In 1841 Pedro II was prematurely declared an adult and crowned emperor.

There is no doubt that Zweig viewed his host country through the rose-tinted glasses of someone who had escaped the horrors of Nazi dominated Europe. In comparison to what happened in the Old World the second biggest country of the New World must have appeared like paradise to him. Here tolerance and peaceful coexistence, of which European intellectuals had dreamt for centuries, seemed to have become a reality. No matter what the racial and cultural origins of those who came to Brazil from Europe, Asia and Africa, they all had become Brazilians and being Brazilian superseded all other differences. This, anyway, is how Zweig saw it.

At the conference I met Edgar and Helga, a couple who taught German language and literature at a university in the south of the country. They were descendants of German and Austrian immigrants and not only did they look "Germanic" but they also spoke perfect German free of any foreign accent. When I asked them if they felt German, Austrian or Brazilian both answered emphatically that they were Brazilians and felt like Brazilians although they were conscious of their Central European heritage that they proudly preserved. Edgar explained to me that Brazil was a racially mixed society without racial prejudices. He was proud of this and confirmed what Stefan Zweig had written about the country. However, when I asked him how he would feel if his daughter married a black man, he admitted after some hesitation that he might not be very happy! Another member of the conference told me that black people found it more desirable to marry a white person than vice versa. What motivates black persons to marry whites is the desire "to improve the race"!

Brazil is a country of immigrants. The Portuguese colonised it. Many Dutch settled there also. Black slaves came from Africa. In the first half of the 20th century many Italians, Germans and Austrians sought to make a new life there. There was also a substantial influx of people from Lebanon, and about 250,000 Japanese live in Sao Paolo, making it the biggest Japanese community outside of Japan. Most of these Brazilian Japanese have been there for a few generations and no longer speak their original mother tongue. However, they have the right to return to Japan if they wish to do so. When Brazil's economy goes down, which happens frequently in between boom times, many Brazilian Japanese would like to avail of this opportunity, but are unable to do so because they no longer speak Japanese. Japanese and Lebanese immigrants also arrived into many other South American countries.

The president of Peru during the time of the Shining Path was Alberto Fujimori. He was of Japanese extraction and when accused of corruption he fled the country and for a while took refuge in Japan. In Peru he was generally called *El Chino* – the Chinese. Abdalá Jaime Bucaram Ortiz was the son of Lebanese immigrants to Ecuador and in 1996 became president of that country. We have mentioned his mad escapades in chapter 7 on Ecuador.

I mention this because it seems to show that Latin American countries are more accepting of political leaders who do not come from the dominant ethnic group (Portuguese or Spanish). In contrast to this, in the United States, politicians of Hispanic, Lebanese or Japanese extraction or other "ethnic" background have never been elected president and have very little chance of ever making it to the White House. Obama, the first black president appears to have been the exception that proves the rule. After his term of office ended, the "rule" asserted itself with a vengeance in the form of Donald Trump. Perhaps Stefan Zweig was not altogether wrong when he believed that Brazil shows us the way towards a better, i.e., racially, ethnically and culturally more tolerant, future. If he was right, this also applies to other South American countries, in spite of the many other problems they undoubtedly have.

10.2 A dream became reality: Brasilia

In the 1950s the Brazilian government launched a daring project that once again put Brazil on the map as a country of the future. President Kubitschek wanted to encourage people to settle not only by the coast but to move into the empty interior of this vast country. He hoped to achieve this by building a completely new capital city where there had been nothing before. It was to be called Brasilia. When I was in high school, I saw a documentary film about the work in progress of that futuristic dream. I remember, in particular, the wonderful buildings made of reinforced concrete seemingly defying the laws of gravity. I was gobsmacked. It must have been every architect's dream to be involved with that project. In April 1960 Brasilia replaced Rio de Janeiro as the capital.

In the autumn of 2004 I was visiting Brazil for the second time. This time Ursula came with me. When I attended a conference of ALEG the previous year, I had not found the time to visit Brasilia. Now I had the opportunity to do so. Theo H, a friend and former colleague of mine in the German Department of University College Dublin, held a position in the university there. On 5th November he awaited us at the airport, escorted us to our hotel and acted as our guide during our stay. Brasilia with her 2.6 million inhabitants cannot match the style and size of Rio de Janeiro with her 7 million inhabitants. But it is an interesting and well-functioning place. In the middle of the 20th century the planners thought that the future belonged to the motorcar and they made Brasilia a city for the car. It is difficult to manage life there if one is not motorised. This is obviously considered to be a disadvantage today, but back then it seemed the correct plan to pursue. Theo recommended that we should hire a car and we followed his advice.

Oskar Niemeyer was the architect of the breath taking representative buildings that I had first seen in the documentary film. Now I saw them for real: the Cathedral, shaped like a crown of thorns, the Brazilian National Congress, the Palacio da Alvarado and the Brazilian National Stadium. Lúcio Costa was responsible for the overall layout of the city. He planned the city to resemble an aeroplane. In the body are situated the businesses and hotels, and the government buildings in the cockpit. The living quarters are located in the wings. There are no street names. One finds the areas, districts and sections of the city by following letters and numbers. Odd numbers are on side, even numbers on the other. In theory it should be very easy to find one's way around by car. In practice it is more difficult, especially after having drunk a few *caipirinhas*. The living quarters are divided into sections, each of which has shops and areas for relaxation (playgrounds, restaurants and so on). There should be no need to travel far for one's shopping and entertainment as everything is close at hand, mostly within walking distance.

I have just mentioned the Brazilian national cocktail. To make a *caipirinha* you need the following; lime, cane sugar, cachaça (distilled spirit made of fermented sugarcane juice) and ice cubes. Cut a lime into wedges, put them into a glass and add cane sugar to taste (I take about a table spoon). Let the wedges sit for a minute or two and then crush them with a pestle until all the juice has been extracted. Leave the crushed lime in the glass. Add ice cubes and top up with two ounces of cachaça. Stir well and drink through a straw. If you order this cocktail in a bar or restaurant be patient as it takes some time to make it. It is well worth waiting for and, in my opinion, much better than the somewhat similar and better-known Cuban *Mojito*.

Going out for meals in Brazil is great fun. Apart from restaurants like those everywhere in the world, there are two uniquely Brazilian institutions. One of them is the *quilo*. Quilo means kilogram. The quilos are self-service restaurants. You fill up your plate with whatever you want and pay according to weight. A kilo of meat and a kilo of salad cost the same. It is a bit like the Viennese *Heuriger* where you go to a counter and have your food weighed. However, in Vienna they waste a lot of time by separately weighing the meat and the salad and the vegetables. The Brazilian model is more efficient. Maybe one day I will succeed in convincing some owners of the Viennese *Heurigen* to adopt the system of the Brazilian *quilos*. As Brazil has a big Japanese community sushi and other Japanese specialities are popular. Many *quilos* have a section with Japanese food. The other uniquely Brazilian kind of restaurant is the *rodizio*. When entering you pay a fixed amount. You choose a table and then proceed to the buffet where you help yourself to vegetables, salads, rice, potatoes etc. At your table you find tokens. One side of each token is green, the other red. Waiters pass by with different cuts of meat. Showing the green side of the token means that you are ready to be served. The red side indicates to the waiter that you are not interested in what he offers you. Once you know the system you will let the inferior cuts pass by and concentrate on the high-quality cuts. All these restaurants are fully licenced.

It may well be that I would miss the stunning environment of Rio, the historic patinas of Petropolis and Paraty or the excitement of the megacity Sao Paolo if I were to live in Brasilia. My friend Theo seemed to be happy there. Brasilia is certainly worth a visit. It is the result of one of the great social and architectural experiments of the 20th century. Without seeing it one cannot really understand what Brazil is all about.

10.3 Fortaleza

If you look for a place with excellent restaurants, wonderful beaches and plenty of sunshine but which is different from the usual resorts in Spain, then fly to Fortaleza. Ursula and I were there in 2004 when I was on my lecture tour. Since my duties were not very time consuming, we were able to enjoy ourselves. The German Lektor assigned by the German Academic Exchange Service (DAAD) to the university put us up in the Hotel Vela de Mar very close to the promenade by the sea.

Sitting on the terrace and drinking our caipirinhas we were accosted by a boy of about ten years of age asking us for money. He addressed me by "Hello, mister!" Although we were advised not to do this, we gave him a few coins. The next day he turned up with another boy, who may have been his brother and again we gave him something. After that he and some of his friends turned up whenever we were sitting on the terrace. They were quite well mannered and had a natural charm. In no way were they obnoxious and their English was surprisingly good. As it was very unlikely that they had the benefit of a formal education they must have picked it up from the tourists. They obviously were very intelligent and they could have achieved a lot in their lives if they had the advantage of a secure home and a sound education.

On Sunday we followed the DAAD-Lektors's recommendation and went on a tour of *Morro Branco* and *Praia dos Fontes*, two superb beaches not far from Fortaleza. We were the only gringos on the bus and we asked the tour guide if she would translate her explanations into Spanish, which she promised to do. She honoured her promise in a fashion; after each cascade of Portuguese words lasting some ten minutes she gave a ten-word rendering in Spanish. The tour was highly enjoyable. We did an exciting buggy ride in the dunes and walked through dramatic canyons formed by compacted sand. Walking through the canyons we were befriended by a Brazilian veterinary surgeon, Luiz, his wife, Carla, and a young friend of theirs, Luciana. They were a lot younger than us and we must have appeared very ancient to them because they took it upon themselves to mind us at every step. Whenever we were scrambling up or down a steep slope or had to step over a gap, Luiz, Carla or Luciana took us by the arm and made sure that we would not fall and break a limb. They were very kind and did not know that we were used to walking and climbing in the Alps.

We returned to Fortaleza in the late afternoon and went to dinner with the Austrian Consul and her husband. The German Lektor was also invited, as was a professor of law from another Brazilian university. We asked the consul about her work. She told us that apart from looking after Austrian business interests a lot of her time was taken up assisting Austrians who were put into jail after being caught, having committed child sexual abuse. There were direct flights between Vienna and Fortaleza and, unfortunately, this attracted a certain percentage of this unwelcome kind of tourists. It was one of the consul's duties to help those who got into trouble with the Brazilian law by making sure that they got the appropriate legal representation.

Ursula had a distant cousin, John, who lived in the municipality of Caucaia near Fortaleza. He was a Redemptorist priest from Wexford in Ireland, who had come to Brazil as a young man and had lived there ever since. We were invited to lunch in his house, which he shared with three fellow priests. The house was spacious and comfortable and it was surrounded by a big walled garden. Two gigantic *dogos argentines*, Argentinian mastiffs, were there to guard the property. Their names were Loboninho (Wolf) and Tigri (Tiger). The priests had decided to get them after an armed robber escaping from the police, jumped over the garden wall and climbed a tree to hide. He was caught and escorted away in handcuffs. I do not think that the priests had spent much time training these huge dogs so that they could fulfil their duty of frightening off intruders. Lobonhinho and Tigri were spoiled and pampered and very gentle creatures and would probably have welcomed any burglar with a friendly lick.

John told us that his order sent him to Rio de Janeiro when he was newly ordained. There he was given a crash course in Portuguese and after a few weeks he was transferred to a remote outpost in the Amazonian rainforest where he spent some twenty years. He remembered that the humidity of the air slowly destroyed his clothes, his books, and the houses the priests lived in. He was lucky that he survived his time there in good health. When he was offered a parish in Fortaleza, he considered himself very lucky. The dry climate, living near the sea, and, most importantly, being back in civilization was like paradise. Much of his work and that of his colleagues in the parish of Caucaia consisted of marrying young couples, who got divorced a year later and in baptizing children born both in and out of wedlock.

We asked him about the political situation in the parish and he told us the following: in the last local elections, the ruling party made the most extravagant promises ranging from free healthcare to free water and electricity to free housing for everybody. The party was promptly re-elected, but as it had plundered the coffers of the municipality of Caucaia to finance its election campaign, there was not a penny left to fulfil even the most modest of their promises.

10.4 The favelas of Rio de Janeiro

In November 2004 Ursula and I and our friend Eileen from Dublin, who joined us with her husband in Rio de Janeiro, mustered up enough courage to book a hang-gliding flight over the city. We had attempted paragliding in the Austrian Alps some years before, but after we had received instructions and a pep talk from our guides and were all ready to jump into the abyss, it was called off because the thermals were not right. In Rio de Janeiro, so we were told, the conditions for paragliding and hang gliding were perfect most of the time. We were driven to a hilltop and brought to a ramp overlooking part of the city near the Atlantic coast. Each of us was to fly in tandem with a pilot. We were instructed to run the length of the ramp and then jump out into the void. It was impressed on us that under no circumstances must we stop running as this would slow the momentum and cause us to dip dangerously once we had jumped off the end of the ramp. We followed the instructions to the letter and took off successfully. It was a leap of faith. We were only in the air for twenty minutes before landing on the beach, but those twenty minutes were incredibly exciting. During the flight we saw a huge sprawling settlement beneath us, between forest-covered hills, the sea and the beach. Later when we tried to find this settlement on the map, we could not see it. The map showed a blank. We had flown over a *favela* (a shanty town).

Although the favelas make up about one third of Rio's population, they officially do not exist. Many favelas started as makeshift shacks without plumbing, sanitation and electricity. There was no planning permission. The living conditions were dreadful. As time went on some of the favelas got organised and managed to steal electricity and improve the living conditions. The authorities finally realised that they could not ignore these settlements completely, and even provided some of them with electricity and plumbing. The favelas are run by drug cartels whose bosses live there themselves albeit in grander houses. All comings and goings are closely watched at all times. The favelas are no-go areas. The police only enter if absolutely necessary, and taxi drivers refuse to take customers there.

However, certain streets are open to outsiders. From what we were told, in the evenings these streets are full of expensive cars, driven by expensive people, who shop for their supply of recreational drugs. Every so often one drug cartel attempts to take over a favela from a rival cartel. When that happens, the police move in to keep the two gangs apart and prevent an all-out war. Favelas are a state within the state and form an important part of the economy of Brazil's big cities. Many of the favela dwellers work in services. A large proportion of hotel porters, waiters, cleaning ladies, messenger boys and others live there. The pay they receive may seem very little to us but for them it is a lot. The relationship between the areas shown on the map and those that officially do not exist is mutually beneficial.

Some favelas have developed into semi-respected and semi-recognized communities. Rocinha and Vila Canoa can be visited by booking a guided tour. Part of what the tourists pay goes to the drug lords and part benefits community projects like schools, hospitals and the like. At least so we were assured. About 100,000 people live in Rocinha, which according to Wikipedia has "developed from a shanty town into an urbanised slum" and is now classified as a *favela bairro*, a favela neighbourhood. We went on a tour of Rocinha and were surprised to find a McDonalds, banks with ATM machines, bus routes, chemists and a lot of other shops. Our guide pointed to a big house outside the favela but very close to its boundary. It belonged, she informed us, to Ivo Pitanguy, a world famous plastic surgeon, who had operated on Niki Lauda after his horrific racing car accident. Silvio Berlusconi and Mummar Gaddafi also counted among his clients. Because he carried out weekly operations in the favela free of charge his house was safe from attacks and robberies. He died in 2016.

Many middle class and upper class homes were situated surprisingly close to the favelas. We were told about a school in one of these upmarket areas close to Rocinha that got caught up in cross fire between rival gangs forcing the kids and teachers to hide under the benches until it was over. The evening after our visit to Rocinha we had dinner in an excellent *rodizio* and afterwards strolled in the direction of Ipanema to our hotel. Suddenly a young man came running at us from behind and tried to snatch Ursula's handbag. Although there was nothing of worth in it, she instinctively held on to it with all her might. The robber let go and ran away. He probably lived in one of the favelas.

Rio is famous for the carnival with its spectacular samba dancing displays. The various communities of the city compete with each other for producing the most colourful and extravagant samba show. There are special samba schools that spend the whole year training for the carnival. Not surprisingly, the best of these can be found in the favelas. Our hotel offered an evening tour to one of these schools. While we sat at our table and drank our caipirinhas, fantastic looking and scantily dressed ladies crowded in on us dancing to an ear deafening dissonant brass band music. Althhough this was interesting enough, we would have liked to return to the hotel after about two hours. However, we had to wait until our guide was ready to pick us up.

On the way back to the hotel the driver asked us if we would like to see some of the transvestite prostitutes for whom Rio was famous. Everybody agreed and he drove us to the area where the transvestites were looking for customers. The transvestites were stunningly beautiful and exuded an almost uncanny femininity.

Canyons of Morro Branco

The summer palace of the Emperor of Brazil

Paraty

Samba dancer

Chapter 11: Africa 2003

11.1 Moshi and Mount Meru

Physically fit hill-walkers who have no climbing experience and are not accustomed to using rope, crampons and ice axe, have a good chance of reaching the summit of Kilimanjaro. At 5,895 m, Kilimanjaro is the highest mountain on the African continent. Depending on the route one chooses, it takes between six and eight days to get to the top and back. Although the long ascent is conducive to acclimatization, altitude sickness can strike at any time. This has nothing to do with fitness. It can happen to anyone.

Many European and American agencies offer guided tours on Kilimanjaro. Although they employ local guides and porters, most of their profit leaves the country. When Ursula and I went to Tanzania in July 2003 with six friends from our two Irish hiking clubs, we engaged a local firm based in Moshi. The owner was E, who also ran a hostel with the beautiful name *Rose Home*. On Monday, 7th July, he awaited us at Kilimanjaro International Airport in Moshi and drove us to his hostel. The following day he organized an excursion to the surroundings of the town. We visited the village of Marangu from where the Coca Cola Route to Kilimanjaro begins and had a picnic at a picturesque waterfall. It was a relaxing day. Ursula and I were in Africa for the first time.

E advised us to ascend 4,562 m high Mount Meru whose summit has the interesting name *Socialist Peak*. This would help us to acclimatise before attempting Kilimanjaro. Many mountaineers travel into neighbouring Kenya and climb Mount Kenya in order to prepare for Africa's highest mountain. Mount Meru is in Tanzania and not far from Kilimanjaro. E's advice made good sense.

On Wednesday we were taken to the Momela Gate, where our five-day hike on Mount Meru began. From the bus we could see water buffaloes, giraffes and monkeys. Our guide was M. He was a mountain guide and ranger and he carried a gun so that he could protect us from the wild animals. While elephants could sometimes turn aggressive, the most dangerous were the water buffaloes. On the first day we walked through thickly vegetated terrain where we saw giraffes, water buffaloes, monkeys and warthogs. Luckily, the water buffaloes did not come too close to us. With the help of my telephoto lens I succeeded in taking a few good pictures of them.

The first hut we stayed in was the Miriakamba Hut. It was well equipped and comfortable. Our cook prepared a good meal and we had enough time for a stroll near the hut to admire the views of Kilimanjaro in the setting sun. M warned us to be careful when visiting the outside toilets at night as elephants and water buffaloes could pose a danger. The next day was cold and humid. We reached the Saddle Hut at 3,000 m above sea level, had our dinner at 5:00 p.m. and went early to bed. We were woken up at midnight and left the hut on Friday, 8th July at 1:00 a.m. for the summit. It was drizzling, but M assured us that the weather would improve later. He was right. After two hours he suffered from a malaria attack and had to return. His assistant guides took over. The higher we climbed the steeper the trail became. The temperature was near 20° C below ziro. Three of our group vomited. By 7:00 a.m. the sun lit up the landscape and it got warmer quickly. We all stood on the summit at 7:45 a.m.

The increasing heat made the descent almost harder than the ascent. Now we could see the way we had come. It was a harsh and bleak landscape that unfolded in front of our eyes. Mount Meru is an extinct volcano. Nothing grows on the grey ash. Around midday we were back at Saddle Hut. After a short rest we started our descent to the Miriakamba Hut where we spent the last night on the mountain. On the final day of our walk, we got dangerously close to some water buffaloes. M chased them away with his whistle. Just as well that he did not have to use the gun!

We had thought about how to distribute the tips to the various guides and porters. The custom was to hand over the complete tip to the head guide together with a note specifying how much each person should get. Nobody knew if he would do as instructed. We were in the middle of discussing this when one of the porters approached us and handed us the following note:

> Dear Sir,
> We eight Porters we don't believe our Ranger about the tip. So, what we asking you Sir is to put forward your tip directly to Porters not indirect through him. We will appreciate highly,
> Remind Sir, Porters
> Please: try to keep secret. So, he should not know about this message.

This confirmed our concerns. But what should we do? We respected M and did not wish to offend him. On the other hand, we wanted to make sure that everybody received his due. We were confronted with the same problem international organisations have when giving aid to developing countries. It is difficult to bypass the authorities of the country in question and deliver the aid directly to the people or communities in need. The authorities, however, cannot always be trusted to administer the aid in a fair way. Finally, we formed a small delegation and asked M if we could tip the porters, cooks and guides directly. To our surprise he agreed. He even offered to hold a little ceremony during which everybody was to be called up and be given the tip by our treasurer. He kept his word and he performed the ceremony very graciously. Of course, we gave him a good tip.

By lunchtime on Saturday, 12th July, we were back in Rose Home. Now we had two and a half days to explore Moshi and find some decent coffee shops and restaurants. There was hardly any car traffic. The streets were not paved and very sparsely lit at night. Going out for a meal in the evenings and coming back we had to bring along our head torches as if we were still on Mount Meru. People were friendly. However, when I took photographs of women assembling outside a building, a soldier warned me that taking pictures was forbidden because this was a military building. He threatened to take the film out of my camera. Luckily, I succeeded in persuading him not to do this. Looking for restaurants we tried our best to find a place that offered genuine African cuisine but had little success. We finally opted for a restaurant that was called *Bristol Cottages* and was run by an elderly English couple. It became our regular during our stay.

On Sunday some of the group wanted to attend Mass. We decided that we all should go. When the staff of Rose Home heard about our plan, two girls were asked to accompany us. The service was completely different from what we were used to. The church was packed. All wore their best clothes and sang with great enthusiasm. It was a most joyful event the like of it I have never experienced in any church in Europe.

11.2 Mount Kilimanjaro

On Tuesday, 15th July we began our ascent of Kilimanjaro. We had opted for the Machame Route. It takes seven days, which is more time than the other routes require, thus giving the hiker a better chance to acclimatise. Instead of overnighting in huts we slept in tents. Our guide was the cook who had fed us so well on Mount Meru.

The first difficulty arose when the bus that drove us to the start got bogged down in the mud. We had to walk the remaining few hundred metres. Registration took an eternity. Finally, we got the green light to start marching. We did not need guides for the first section. By following the obvious path, we should reach the first camp in a few hours. The porters carried our tents and some of our own equipment so that we were left with only our light daypacks. Because of heavy rain in the past days the trail had turned into a sea of mud. We were used to wading in the boggy terrain of the Irish mountains, but this was worse than anything we had ever encountered at home. At least we wore good hiking boots and gaiters. The poor porters, however, walked in sandals. Instead of rucksacks they carried huge plastic bags. Because we were not the only group walking to the campsite, an endless stream of porters passed us by at top speed slithering and sliding all over. Some fell into the muck. It was heart breaking to see how these poor people had to toil for the likes of us.

Mary K and I were the first to arrive at the campsite. It was seven o'clock and dark. The site was enormous and full of people. Nobody knew anything about our group. We knocked at the door of a little hut where a few porters were eating their dinner. They had no idea where our group was, but kindly invited us to share their dinner with them, which we thankfully declined. After an hour or so we found our guides and our tents. By 9:00 p.m. we were all in our sleeping bags and received our dinner. It was Ursula's first time in a tent. She was not exactly enthused.

The next day the sun was shining, the paths were dry and we had wonderful views. Shira Camp at 4,500 m above sea level was a relief compared to the chaos of the previous night. In order to get to Barranco Camp the following day we had to descend a few hundred metres. Oddly enough, it was at Barranco Camp that I suffered from a bout of altitude sickness. I could not move my fingers and had difficulty formulating words. Several cups of tea and a few hours rest restored me fairly quickly. As far as the scenery was concerned this was the best day. The views of the summit of Kilimanjaro and of the Arrow Glacier were most impressive. On Friday, 18th July, we overnighted in the Karanga Valley. The way there was short and easy and we all felt in top form. The last camp before the summit attempt was Barangu Camp, at 4,600 m above sea level. It is a bleak place without vegetation. The only living creatures apart from us were big black crows. On our left (as we were facing the summit of Kilimanjaro) was a huge drop beyond which we could see Mount Meru very far away and very small. Turning to the right we had a view of Mawenzi, at 5,149 m third highest mountain in Africa.

We had ample of time for rest. This was a good thing because we had to start our push for the summit shortly after midnight on Monday, 20th July. The sky was clear, there was a half moon and the temperature was 20° C below zero. The glaciers of Kilimanjaro were shimmering in the moonlight. When the sun rose, the temperature rose quickly too. A few hundred metres before reaching the summit Ursula got sick. I was worried about her and we all advised her to descend with one of the assistant guides, which she did after some deliberation. I then continued with the others to the top. At 9:30 a.m. we stood on the summit of Kilimanjaro. On other comparable occasions I was on a high. This time I felt nothing but disappointment because Ursula was not with me.

During our descent we once again spent a good bit of time deciding on how to dish out the tips. Unfortunately, our guide was not as cooperative as M had been. He was not prepared to deviate from the established custom of collecting the total amount. We had no choice but to hand him over the money together with the instructions how to distribute it. As soon as he had the money, he disappeared. He remained absent when we were handed our certificates. E was waiting for us with his bus. All the porters and assistant guides were still there. We told them what each of them should receive from the guide but will never know if they got their fair share.

As is so often the case on my travels, the journey turned out to be more rewarding than the destination. Our destination was the summit of Kilimanjaro. But my best memories are of Mount Meru, E and the friendly people in Rose Home and in Moshi. And then there was the joyful church service on Sunday, 13th July 2003.

View of Kilimanjaro from Mount Meru

In the village of Marangu

Chapter 12: Argentina

12.1 Córdoba and Buenos Aires

The year after I retired, I had the opportunity to give guest lectures in different universities in Argentina, in the autumn of 2006. I had received invitations from the German departments of Córdoba, Buenos Aires and La Plata and as we now enjoyed unlimited free time, Ursula and I decided to spend about six weeks in that country. My idea was to lecture a day or two in each university and to have a holiday for the rest of the time. However, I soon had to accept that my hosts had different ideas. Each of them asked me to give a week's course involving a few hours every day. This was more than I had bargained for, but it gave us the opportunity to experience a bit more of life in Argentina.

Our first destination was the historic Spanish colonial city of Córdoba, with about 1.3 million inhabitants the second biggest city of the country. The National University of Córdoba goes back to a Jesuit foundation of 1613 and is Argentina's oldest university, part of which has been declared a World Heritage Site by UNESCO. Our host was the professor of German. He had come from Germany to Argentina when he was still a young man. The parents of one of the lecturers in the department, Brigitte Merzig, had left Germany for Argentina in the 1950s in search for a better life. Whatever their hopes may have been, they certainly had been affected by the various political and financial crises the country had gone through, most of all by the collapse of the financial system in 2001/2002. Nevertheless, the professor and his wife lived in a comfortable house in a pleasant neighbourhood and Brigitte and her family had an apartment in Córdoba and a weekend house by the coast. The Kirchner government had brought about some stability and was slowly paying back what had been taken from the citizens in the course of the crash of 2001/2002. Now the economy was booming again and life was beginning to improve, but journeys to Europe or the United States were still well-nigh impossible for most Argentinians due to the poor exchange rate of the *peso*.

We enjoyed our week in Córdoba. I spent four afternoons teaching, which meant that we had enough time to explore the city. We found some excellent restaurants that served superb steaks for which Argentina is well known. My favourite cut was *bife chorizo*. I am not sure what the European equivalent would be. It may have been a rib eye steak.

Walking around the historic part of the city we came across a travel agent who had a very special offer; a return bus journey from Córdoba to the Iguazu Waterfalls and three nights in a hotel on the Brazilian side, all for hundred twenty dollars per person. The dates were 13th – 17th October. We were to go to Buenos Aires in a few days but as we intended to pass through Córdoba again in a few weeks, we decided on the spur of the moment to book the trip. The price was extremely good value. We were therefore dumbstruck when we learned that it was given in Argentinian pesos. This meant that the whole package cost even less than we had thought. I will come back to this trip later.

In the same travel agency, we spotted an advertisement for a guided hike to a canyon in the *Parque Nacional Quebrada Condorito* where one could see condors in flight. We were told that the hike would last about four hours and required a good level of physical fitness. We booked it for the next day. Before paying we were asked to sign a lengthy disclaimer that outlined the many potential dangers. Reading that document made us wonder if we were able for this adventure, but as we were both experienced hill-walkers, we took the chance.

The following morning, we and a few other gringos were driven to the National Park and started to hike. No one in the group looked like an experienced hill-walker or mountaineer. They came from the Netherlands, USA and Germany. All of them had travelled all over the world, mostly by using organised trips, and they were so busy telling each other where they had been that they hardly noticed where they were at the moment. They reminded me of a dinner guest in the house of one of my Irish friends who was an excellent cook. Throughout the dinner he kept reminiscing about the wonderful meals he had enjoyed in famous restaurants all over the world. He hardly noticed what he was eating.

The National Park is situated within the Argentinian Pampas. We walked on level ground to the rim of a huge canyon from where we got a glimpse of a few big birds a good distance away. The guide told us that they were condors. The point at the rim of the canyon is called *Balcón Sur*. The hike was totally harmless. If we had rented a car, we could have driven there ourselves and walked without a guide.

After finishing my lectures in Córdoba, we took a seven-hour bus journey to Buenos Aires, where we arrived on the evening of Sunday 17th September. The Austrian ambassador, Dr Gudrun Graf, and her husband Bernd had very kindly offered to put us up in their residence during our stay. The professor of German in the University of Buenos Aires wanted me to give a one-week course, the details and times of which were to be arranged on arrival.

We took a taxi from the bus terminal to the ambassadorial residence. It was a warm evening and just getting dark. Driving through the wide boulevards and passing by the monumental buildings we immediately got a good feeling about Buenos Aires. Some cities put an instant spell on the visitor before he or she has had the chance of establishing an informed opinion. It is like love at first sight.

Arriving at the embassy in a somewhat dishevelled state, after our long bus ride, the two sons of our hosts played a piano piece for four hands to welcome us. They were in their early teens and of exceptional abilities. Not only were they accomplished musicians but also excellent linguists. They spoke German, English, French and Spanish. Dr Graf and her husband had worked out a wonderful programme of evening entertainments for us. There was an evening at the opera in the famous Teatro Colon, a visit to an exhibition and a dinner in the embassy with friends. It all sounded absolutely superb.

The next morning, I rang the professor of German in order to discuss my timetable. As it turned out there was nothing to discuss. I was to teach in the university every evening from 7:00 p.m. to 9:00 p.m. My students were mature students who worked during the day and attended classes in the evenings. The journey to the university took an hour by underground. So that was it! I was free all day but had to sing for my bread and butter in the evening. Bye-bye to the Teatro Colon, bye-bye to the opening of the exhibition and to the dinner with friends! I had to work, but Ursula was free to enjoy everything the ambassador had arranged.

Dutifully I left the residence by 6:00 p.m. and laboured away till 9:00 p.m. When Ursula was not otherwise engaged in the evenings, she took the underground and met me after my lecture in a coffee house. One evening the professor and her husband took us out for dinner in a restaurant near the university. The students were stunning. I was very impressed by their general knowledge and enthusiasm. They made me wonder if I had taken the right decision to go into retirement three years before I had to.

When the ambassador took Ursula to the Teatro Colon and to the opening of the exhibition the procedure was as follows: they would walk from the house through the kitchen into the garage and enter the chauffeur-driven Mercedes with bulletproof windows. The security door of the garage opened automatically and out they drove. Dr Graf impressed upon Ursula that when stopping outside the theatre or the gallery they would walk swiftly, no delay and no chatting to friends was allowed. There was great concern about security. Kidnappings of members of well-to-do and important families were a daily occurrence. The families of ambassadors were popular targets. One very common kind of kidnapping was the so-called *secuestro express*, which literally means express kidnapping. The criminals would abduct your child or wife or husband and ask for ten thousand dollars. You paid that and the abducted person was instantly released. It all was over in a very short time. Ten thousand dollars was a handsome sum, but most targeted families could easily afford it. Some of the ambassador's friends had been victims of a *secuestro express* and she had no desire to become one too.

As Ursula and I did not fall into the category of potential targets of an express kidnapping we felt quite safe. Both of us moved around the city by bus and underground, sometimes the two of us together, at other times on our own. We never encountered a problem. Buenos Aires with her wide boulevards and the abundance of coffee houses felt like a synthesis of Paris and Vienna.

A few times we went to the *Plaza de Mayo* on the eastern side of which the *Casa Rosada*, the presidential palace, is situated. Now it was all peace and quiet and it was hard to imagine the chaotic scenes that had taken place there six years earlier, at the height of the financial crisis in 2001. When it was rumoured that the banks were about to crash, people started to withdraw their money. The banks panicked and reacted by freezing the accounts. On 20th December 2001 violent protests forced President Fernando de la Rua to resign. He had to be airlifted out of the *Casa Rosada* by helicopter to escape the angry crowd that threatened to lynch him. Later it became known that the banks had warned their big clients (rich Argentinians and international firms) of their precarious situation and allowed them to withdraw their money or to transfer it abroad. As always, it was the middle classes who bore the brunt of the government's corruption and pathetic policies.

While the financial crisis of 2001/2002 seemed to be almost forgotten in the new boom times, other horrors of the past were still remembered. Every Thursday a big demonstration took place in front of the Casa Rosada led by the mothers of those who disappeared during the military dictatorship between 1976 and 1983. In those years many people who opposed or were suspected of opposing the government were kidnapped, tortured and killed. The campaign against these dissidents was called Operation Condor and backed by the United States of America. The mothers of the disappeared called themselves *Madres de la Plaza de Mayo* and started their demonstrations in 1977 defying a government ban on demonstrations. They paid dearly for this. The leader of the group, Azucena Villaflor who had published the names of the disappeared in a newspaper was kidnapped, tortured and murdered by being thrown out of an airplane. Two French nuns who supported the movement suffered the same fate. When we were in Buenos Aires almost thirty years after these events, the mothers of the disappeared were still holding their demonstrations every Thursday. Their political agenda had become wider. They were now demonstrating for a more equal society holding up banners demanding *distribución de la riqueza ya!* – Distribution of wealth now!

After finishing my work in Buenos Aires, I had another week of lecturing ahead of me in La Plata.

12.2 La Plata

La Plata, a town of approximately 80,000 inhabitants is an hour's bus ride south east of Buenos Aires. Our host was Professor Graciela Wamba, and once again I was engaged in lecturing every day for one week. As the classes took place in the early afternoon, we had the mornings and the evenings to explore this pleasant city at leisure. Our hotel was only a twenty-minute walk from the university. La Plata prides itself as the home of the country's most important theatre and opera house after the Teatro Colon in Buenos Aires.

The old *Teatro Argentino de La Plata* burnt down in 1977 and the new building that replaced it was opened in 1999. The "brutalist" style of the architect Wimpy Tomas Oscar García does not appeal to everybody. However, the interior is stunningly beautiful in its simplicity and the acoustics are superb, as we experienced when our host took us there to a ballet evening.

Ursula and I got into the habit of meeting after my lectures in a charming Viennese style café on the way from the hotel to the university. During our stay the town was "invaded" by a protesting crowd of the so-called "dispossessed". For a few days they caused chaos by blocking roads with burning car tyres. To feed the fires some climbed onto the roofs of bus shelters so that they could break branches of the trees that lined the boulevards. Sometimes the roofs of the shelters collapsed under the weight of the protesters. To say that the police kept a low profile would be an understatement. The guardians of the peace were completely invisible. They probably felt that confronting the protesters would only make the situation worse.

Sitting at our table by the window, sipping coffee and eating delicious pastries we looked in amazement at the mayhem outside. Graciela told us that the dispossessed were people who had lost their homes, after being driven off the land by the landlords. As a consequence, they had developed a nomadic life style similar to that of the Romany people or the travelling community in Ireland. She was a bit vague about the history of the dispossessed. When did these events happen? Did those we saw protesting belong to the first generation of the dispossessed or were they the heirs of events that happened a long time ago? Nobody seemed to know. It was hard to make out what exactly they were demonstrating against or for. Some of them held up posters asking for the legalisation of abortion, but we had the feeling that this was just an excuse for showing their general discontent with the system they blamed for their situation. It seemed that the locals were well used to this kind of disruption. Nobody in the café paid much attention and nobody seemed to be worried or afraid.

A professor of sociology published a long article in a newspaper defending the culture of the dispossessed and arguing against their discrimination. This reminded me of the situation of the travelling people in Ireland who, it has been said, are the successors of people who were dispossessed during the famine in the 19th century. Although the Irish travellers have recently been given the status of a separate ethnic group, the fact is that they differ from the rest of the population of Ireland only in that they have kept any foreign blood away by exclusively marrying amongst themselves, which, at least in theory, makes them the purest of all Irish!

Wandering about the town we came across a statue of Irishman William Brown, the founder of the Argentinian navy. He was born in Foxford, County Mayo, Ireland in 1777 and played an important role in the fight for independence from Spain and in various wars with Brazil and Uruguay. He defeated a Uruguayan fleet on the River Paraná that was commanded by Giuseppe Garibaldi. The future Italian freedom hero was imprisoned and threatened with execution. It was thanks to the intervention of William Brown that Garibaldi was released. Brown died in 1857 and is buried in the La Recoleta cemetery in Buenos Aires. In 2012 the William Brown Memorial Park, with a statue of the admiral was opened in his native Irish village of Foxford.

12.3 Salta

We returned from La Plata to Buenos Aires, where we met up with our Irish friend, Eileen. From Buenos Aires to Salta, it is a 1,500 km long bus trip in a north-north-westerly direction. We left Buenos Aires in the early afternoon and arrived in Salta the following morning. As always, the bus ride was comfortable and uneventful. The main reason for going there was to see the canyons of the Chalchaqui valleys between Salta and the wine growing area around Cafayte. In Salta we found a travel agency that offered tours to Cafayate and back, in one day, including some walks in the canyons and a wine tasting session. From the information we were given we figured that the "walks" consisted of leaving the bus for a few minutes and looking at some feature of interest close to the road. What we wanted was a proper hike through the canyons but this option was not available.

So, we decided to rent a car and to drive to Cafayate the next day. The main problem was to negotiate the Naples like traffic chaos out of the city. Once we had left Salta behind, we enjoyed a stunning 190 km drive on an empty road. We passed by canyons and mountains of fantastic rock formations with Grand Canyon like reddish colorations. Some of the formations have been given evocative names like *Garganta del Diablo,* the throat of the devil, Amphitheatre, Toad etc. We arrived in Cafyate in the early afternoon and were lucky to find a guide in the local tourist office. He charged the three of us a total of twenty dollars for taking us on an unforgettably spectacular walk over the tops of small hills, into dry canyons, caves and through shallow rivers. In the three hours we spent in the vast expanse of this strange and wonderful landscape we did not see anybody. How privileged we were to have all this entirely to ourselves!

Salta has a museum that is well worth a visit. The *Museo de Arqueologia de Alta Montana de Salta* (MAAM) is in possession of three mummies of children who were sacrificed to the Gods by the Incas about five hundred years ago. They were discovered on 16th March 1999, by an archaeological team led by the American anthropologist Johan Reinhard. Their remains were found near the summit of the 6,739 m high *Llullaillaco* volcano on the border between Chile and Argentina, in the Atacama Desert. Because of the extreme dryness of the air and the high altitude, the *Children of Llullaillaco* are exceptionally well preserved. They have been dubbed *la doncella,* the maiden, *la niña del rayo,* the lightning girl, and *el niño,* the boy. It is believed that they were given drugs to put them asleep before they were placed inside a small chamber where they were left to die. *El niño* was approximately seven years old. He was tied up, possibly because he resisted. The two girls, whose DNA suggests that they were half-sisters, did not seem to have caused any difficulties to the people who took them there, as they show no signs of a struggle. Lightning damaged the shoulder of the six years old *niña del rayo* after she had died. The most famous of the three mummies is that of the fifteen years old *doncella* or *Maiden of Llullaillaco.* Experts believe that she was a Sun Virgin and that she was chosen at the age of ten to become a sacrifice to the Gods in order to ensure the wellbeing of her community.

The mummies are exhibited regularly in the museum. Only one mummy can be seen at a time. We were there in 2006 when *la doncella* was on exhibit. Looking at the remains of that poor girl was a very strange experience. I was deeply moved and at the same time felt I that I should not be looking at all. I was intruding into a mystery that should not be dragged into public view. I understand why some members of the indigenous community have strong reservations about the mummies of the children being put on exhibit. These girls were sacrificed hundreds of years ago to ensure benevolent weather, a rich harvest and good health for their community. According to popular belief, the spirits of these blood victims still watch over their people. Maybe they should have been left to rest in peace where they were buried.

The leader of the archaeological team that uncovered the *Children of Llullaillaco* is an extraordinary man. Johan Reinhard was born in Joliet, Illinois, and studied at the Universities of Arizona, USA and Vienna, Austria, where he received a Ph.D. in anthropology in 1974. He took part in numerous underwater archaeological studies all over the world as well as in excavations in the Alps, the Andes and the Himalayas. Apart from being an expert archaeologist and anthropologist, with an impressive record of scholarly publications, he has been a successful expedition leader, mountaineer and diver. It has been said that he has summited more mountains in the Andes of over 20,000 feet than any other climber. He is an explorer-in-residence at the National Geographic Society, a visiting professor at the Catholic University in Salta, and an honorary professor of the Catholic University of Arequipa in Peru, to name just a few of his honorary positions. Apart from English he speaks Spanish, Nepali, and German.

Reading about somebody like Johan Reinhard, I cannot help feeling some envy. I have achieved a certain degree of proficiency in some foreign languages, learned a bit about history and have hiked and climbed in the Alps and in the Andes but I have done nothing at the level achieved by Johan Reinhard. He is a great all-rounder, an academic who does not confine himself to studying objects sitting behind a desk but who engages in the hard field-work required in his area. On top of all this he is a better mountaineer than many professional guides.

Well, unfortunately, we cannot all be like that. By writing my travel memories I am perhaps trying to convince myself as well as my readers that travelling can be a rewarding activity for ordinary folks also.

12.4 A trip to Iguazu

From Salta we took the bus to Córdoba, where our friend Eileen left us for Mendoza. Ursula and I started the journey to Iguazu that we had booked almost four weeks earlier. The 12th of October is a national holiday in Argentina. It is called *Día del Respeto a la Diversidad Cultural* (Day of Respect for Cultural Diversity), previously *Día de la Raza* (Race Day). The real significance of 12th October is, however, that on that day in 1492 Christopher Columbus landed in the Americas. The Italian explorer was anything but a champion of respectful interaction with other races and cultures. Although the natives showed nothing but friendliness, his quest for gold led him to maltreat and subjugate them brutally. Perhaps the 12th October has been named "Race Day" and later "Day of Respect for Cultural Diversity" in order to make up for the wrongdoings of Columbus and the Spanish *conquistadores*. Because in 2006 that day was a Thursday, Argentinians enjoyed a very long weekend. Our bus trip was a special offer for this extended holiday.

The distance from Córdoba to Iguazu by road is 1,440 km. It took us a night and a full day to reach our destination on the evening of 13th October. We were the only gringos on the bus full of good humoured and friendly Argentinians who in dealing with us showed great respect for cultural diversity. Since the bus moved at a safe speed between 80 and 90 km per hour and kept stopping for food and coffee breaks, we made slow progress. Around midday we had a long break, at a mine where we could buy semiprecious and precious stones for lower prices than in jewellery shops. We were given a tour of the mine that lasted at least an hour. The guide was full of praise for the mining company she worked for. When I asked her how much the miners were paid, she could not or did not wish to give me a figure. We were glad when evening came and we arrived at our hotel on the Brazilian side of the falls, where we relaxed by the swimming pool and had dinner before falling into bed.

The next day we were brought on an extensive tour of the Argentinian side of the Iguazu Falls. I had expected something like the Niagara Falls and did not know that the Iguazu Falls consisted of numerous waterfalls one more dramatic than the other. In spite of the crowds of visitors we enjoyed the tremendous views.

In the afternoon our tour operator took us on an excursion to the Itaipu Dam, a gigantic hydroelectric station on the Paraná River on the border between Brazil and Paraguay. When it was completed in 1984 it was the biggest hydropower station in the world, only to be surpassed in 2008 by the Three Gorges Dam in China. Today the Itaipu power plant has twenty turbines eighteen of which are running constantly allowing two to be shut down for maintenance. Each turbine generates about 700 MW. To give an impression of what this means: the water of all the Iguazu Falls has the capacity to feed only two of these generators!

The Itaipu Dam is a mighty sight indeed that all too easily makes one forget the social and environmental price that had to be paid for this feat of engineering. Ten thousand families living in the vicinity of the Paraná River were moved and the Guaíra National Park was quite literally liquidated. In order to create the Itaipu reservoir, the National Park, including the rock over which the Guaíra Falls poured, was flooded. The Guaíra Falls consisted of seven groups of cataract waterfalls amounting to a total of eighteen falls whose flow rate was among the greatest in the world. Not only were the falls flooded, the rock that created them was blasted away in the interest of easier navigation. This makes any future restoration of the falls impossible.

On 17th January 1982 thousands of tourists came to have a last look at the falls before they disappeared forever. A suspension bridge leading to a viewpoint collapsed and 80 people died. The Brazilian poet Carlos Drummond de Andrade wrote a poignant poem in memory of the Guaíra Falls the translation of which reads:

Here seven visions, seven liquid sculptures
vanished through the computerised calculations
of a country ceasing to be human
in order to become a chilly corporation, nothing more.
A movement becomes a dam.

In the evening a Samba Show was organised for us on the Brazilian side. Wonderfully built half naked black ladies, decorated with fantastic feathers, were dancing on a stage to ear splitting dissonant music (what we call *Katzenmusik* in German: the "music" cats are making when they are "singing"). At this show we were served a meal and given one drink of *caipirinha*. It was similar to what we had seen two years earlier in a samba school in Rio de Janeiro. Two hours would have been perfectly satisfactory. But we had to wait for the bus to bring us back to our hotel. The performance went on till one in the morning. A few times we left our table and went out to get some fresh air. We were not the only ones. Lots of children were playing outside unsupervised while their parents were inside watching the Samba dancing. Some of the children were as young as five and nobody seemed to worry about their safety.

The following day we toured the Brazilian side of the falls. We saw the waterfall that features in the opening scene of the film *The Mission* where native Indians tie a Jesuit missionary to a float and send him down to his death. Being inspired by the bravery of these Jesuits of the 17th century Ursula and I decided to risk a boat tour that was advertised as *La Gran Aventura*. A speedboat drove us right under a big waterfall where we got totally drenched. It was very exciting indeed. My camera got soaked and was out of action for a few days.

Instead of returning by bus to Córdoba, which was included in our price we decided to travel directly from Iguazu to Buenos Aires where we were to meet up with our friend Eileen who we expected by then to be back from Mendoza. We took a taxi from our hotel to the bus terminal on the Argentinian side. When we crossed the border from Brazil into Argentina, I heard the driver say to the customs official that he had two *gringos* in his car who wanted to catch a bus. Now, although in Latin America any foreigner especially if he or she has white skin can be called *gringo* or *gringa*, the term is mostly applied to North Americans. I could not resist telling the driver: *No somos gringos, somos Europeos*. When he asked us where we were from and I replied that I was from Austria he switched to perfect German. His grandparents, he told us, had come from the Hunsrück-region in Rhineland-Palatinate. Here was another example of a Brazilian of immigrant background who had preserved his cultural heritage and the language of his ancestors.

Las madres de la Plaza de Mayo

La Gran Aventura

Chapter 13: The Austrian Alps 2007, 2013 and 2018

13.1 In praise of slowness

The slower one travels the more one takes in. If we accept this premise, walking is the best form of travel. From the Middle Ages to the 19th century young craftsmen gained work experience by staying with different masters, in different parts of their country, from whom they could learn. For a few years they walked from town to town in search of work and to gain experience. Young painters walked from Germany to Italy to study the old masters and to learn new techniques from contemporary Italian colleagues. These years were called *Wanderjahre*. The song cycles *Die schöne Müllerin* and *Die Winterreise* by Franz Schubert and Wilhelm Müller pay tribute to the tradition of *Wandern*. The Romantics used *wandern* as a metaphor for life. Life is a *Wanderung* from birth to death. When I was young, I often thought of walking one of the European *Weitwanderwege*, long distance walks, for example from Vienna to Rome. As I neared retirement age, I toyed with the idea of doing the *Camino de Santiago* from Paris or from Pamplona to Santiago de Compostela. Walking alone would give me plenty of time to reflect on my past life and to plan what to do with the rest of it. I am a little ashamed to admit that I did neither. I was simply too lazy.

Yet, I love walking, especially in the hills and the mountains. Maybe it was the prospect of walking the endless Castilian plains in the Spanish heat, often alongside busy main roads that turned me off from doing the *Camino de Santiago*. In the Alps it is possible to walk long routes by trekking from hut to hut. The huts are between five and eight hours walking time from each other and by availing of them one can spend a few days, a week or longer staying in the mountains without having to descend into a town. Most of the huts today are well equipped and reasonably comfortable. They have showers, facilities for washing cloths and drying wet gear and they provide food and drink. This allows for the luxury of travelling light. The scenery is always spectacular, and one often meets interesting people in the huts.

Yet, walking is not the slowest of movements. Rock climbing is even slower. True, one rarely climbs rocks for longer than a few hours. But there are routes that take a few days and require the climber to bivouac on rock faces. My climbing abilities were far from enabling me to risk such adventures. What I liked were easy, long climbs in big mountains, requiring between one and three hours of walking in and out. There is an important difference between walking in the mountains and rock climbing. While the hiker has time to talk to other people during the walk or to let the mind drift, the rock climber must be totally focused on every move. There is no room for any other thought. It is almost like meditation. My travel diary would be incomplete if I did not include two of my climbing adventures and one long distance hike in the Austrian Alps.

13.2 The Gesäuse National Park

The *Gesäuse National Park* is part of the *Ennstaler Alpen* in the province of Styria, about three hours by car from Vienna. The highest and best-known mountain of the Ennstaler Alpen is the *Hoher Dachstein* near the ski resort of Schladming. The Dachstein Range does not belong to the Gesäuse National Park and has consequently been exploited commercially. A cable car brings tourists up to the glacier at almost three thousand metres above sea level. There is a restaurant, a skywalk and plenty of buzz. Hordes of people walk across the glacier from the cable car station to a hut at the foot of the Hoher Dachstein and back. The ski runs and the ski lifts on the glacier are busy all year round. In contrast to this the Gesäuse is a paradise for those who seek solitude in the mountains. Yes, there are huts and the walker is grateful for the service they offer. But there are no cable cars and no ski lifts. The only way you get to the summits of these magnificent limestone mountains is the hard way; you have to walk or climb. By climbing I mean either scrambling on exposed rock, or proper rock climbing with the help of a rope and other climbing gear or by using a *Klettersteig* (*via ferrata*). I will say more about the via ferratas in chapter 13.4.

The main place in the Gesäuse is the market town of Admont with the splendid Benedictine monastery. Its library was built in 1776 and houses the largest collection of religious literature after the Vatican. On a hill outside the town is the baroque castle Röthelstein. Before it was sold and turned into a hotel it had belonged to the monastery. In August 2017 I spent two weeks there with a group of my Irish hiking friends. In the castle is a small chapel that is still used for special occasions like weddings or baptisms. When some of my group asked me where they could attend mass on Sunday I got in touch with the monastery and asked if one of their priests could say mass for us in the chapel on Saturday evening. To our surprise and delight the abbot came up in person and read mass for us.

For me this was neither my first nor my last visit to the Gesäuse. As it is not too far from Vienna and because it offers everything the alpinist can wish for, I am often there.

13.3 Climbing-adventures

13.3.1 A long alpine traverse 2007

In July 2007 Willi Drofenik, one of my Viennese climbing and hiking friends, and I decided to attempt one of the longest alpine traverses in the Gesäuse. It starts with a two hour-long walk to a hut (the *Haindlkarhütte)*. The next day one has to master a technically easy but very long and exposed climbing route leading via *Rosskuppe* and *Dachl*, to the summit of the *Hochtor*, at 2,369 m the highest mountain of the Gesäuse. Descending via the *Josefinensteig* to another hut, the *Hesshütte*, takes two to three hours. After spending the night there, one faces a descent of four hours via the steep *Wasserfallweg,* back to the car park. In terms of the UIAA (Union Internationale des Associacions de Alpinistes) the degree of difficulty of the climbing route is between 1+ and 2+. Grade 1 is the easiest, grade 3 to 5 are of medium difficulty, 6 to 7 are very hard and anything above is extreme. In theory there is no upper limit, but very few climbers can get beyond 9. From Vienna and back the whole adventure takes three full days.

I took up climbing when I was in my early fifties. Up to then I had only walked in the mountains. I wanted to acquire some climbing techniques and learn how to use a rope because it is not uncommon to come across exposed sections on alpine hikes. I took a few climbing courses in Ireland and practiced with friends what I had learned. What originally was meant to assist me on difficult hikes soon became a passion and for some time I spent more time on rock faces than on mountain paths. Because I was a latecomer to climbing I had to limit myself to the lower climbing grades. This opened a world of new opportunities for me. Near Vienna, in the Hohe Wand, are lots of long climbing routes within my capabilities. I have spent many superb days there. In Ireland the routes are shorter, but because they do not have climbing aids drilled into the rocks they tend to be more challenging. My most important climbing partner and climbing mentor in Ireland is Gerry Moss, a highly experienced old hand on the rocks. Although he is a few years my senior he still can lead any grade 5 climb extremely competently. His friendship has enormously enriched my life in the past decades.

Our first hut, the Haindlkarhütte, was situated in a rather grim looking spot. The surrounding landscape was wild and rocky and rather dark. Yet, inside the hut we felt protected from the hostile elements. The only other guests were two climbers of about our age who told us that they planned to climb the *Jahn Zimmer* route. We were full of admiration. This is a route of medium difficulty, UIAA grade 3+. However, with almost 30 pitches it is extremely long and demands great endurance and very good route-finding skills. The chances of making mistakes and getting lost are considerable. This certainly was above our league. The two fellows were familiar with the route we intended to do the following day. They advised us, that although it was technically not hard and many climbed it free, we should use our rope because there were some seriously exposed sections where one could not afford to make a mistake. They also recommended that we should attempt the *Rossschweif* sometime in the future. This is a long and scenic climb, UIAA between grade 2 and 3, to the summit of the Hochtor.

The next morning, we left the hut at 7:00 a.m. After walking for half an hour, we reached the start of the *Peternpfad*. This is an easy climb/hard scramble (UIAA grades 1 and 2) leading up to the *Peternscharte*, a saddle between two peaks, which we reached at midday. From there we had the option of descending to the Hesshütte in about two or three hours. Turning right we saw the pointed peak of the *Rosskuppe* and in the distance the summit of the Hochtor. As the weather looked stable, we reckoned that we had enough time to complete the tour as planned. However, as is often the case with long alpine routes, even technically easy ones, it took us much longer than we had expected. Part of the reason was that our rucksacks, filled with clothes and provisions for three days, were quite heavy. As I did not know what to expect I had brought too much climbing gear with me. Instead of just packing a few nuts and slings for protection I carried my whole climbing rack.

The views were absolutely spectacular. After the Rosskuppe came the *Dachl* ("roof"), a ridge with a sharp edge, a sheer drop to the right and a sloping slab on the left with good friction that made it easy to walk. Getting to the summit of the Hochtor required more climbing, mostly on good holds and solid foot placements. We reached it at 7:00 p.m., two hours later than we had anticipated. The Josefinensteig by which one descends to the Hesshütte usually takes between two and three hours. As we were tired, weighed down by our heavy rucksacks and as it got dark by 9:00 p.m. it took us three hours. We arrived at the hut at 10:00 p.m. tired but happy. Luckily, there was still food and beer to be had to celebrate our achievement. The hard work was done. The descent via the Wasserfallweg the following morning back to our car was easy peasy in comparison to what we had behind us.

13.3.2 A climb with an exciting finish

We did not forget what the two climbers in the Haindlkarhütte had told us about the Rossschweif. I looked for more information in guidebooks and on the Internet and liked what I found. The climbing route (UIAA difficulty 2 and 3) starts near the Hesshütte at 1,699 m above sea level and ends on the summit of Hochtor at 2,369 m. The climb thus covers almost seven hundred metres. The best way back down to the hut is via the Josefinensteig. Guidebooks and websites describe the route as technically easy but serious because of its length and exposure. They all agree that under no circumstances should one underestimate the dangers and that the climb should only be undertaken in good weather.

Six years went by before we got around to attempt climbing the Rossschweif. Willi and I departed from Vienna on 11th July 2013 at 10 a.m. At 1:20 p.m. we left the car park at the *Kummerbrücke* near Hieflau where we started our hike to the Hesshütte via the Wasserfallweg, a steep and strenuous route especially if one is laden down with a heavy rucksack. We arrived at the hut at 6:00 p.m. ready for a few beers and a hearty meal. We had secured a room just for the two of us. This meant that we could leave some stuff behind that was not needed for the climb as we planned to be back in the evening.

After a good breakfast we left the hut at 8:15 a.m. and made for the start of the climb. Unfortunately, in spite of following the instructions given in our guidebook, we failed to find it. So, we went back to the hut and asked for clearer directions. The directions the hut warden gave us were identical with the ones we had followed before. Apparently, we had not gone far enough. So, off we went again, passed the point where we had returned and after a few more minutes we found the start. It was even marked in red letters: RS! We had lost more than an hour and felt rather foolish. It was now 10 a.m. Putting on our gear took about half an hour. We finally started climbing at 10:30 a.m.

The Rossschweif is a ridge climb whose semi-circle shape does indeed remind one of a horsetail (this is what Rossschweif literally means). For the first two hours we were moving on a wide ridge on somewhat gritty slabs. This was easy enough and we did not need to use the rope. After that the character of the route changed. The ridge became very narrow and the exposure was dramatic. However, there were blocky handholds, little turrets and good footsteps.

We now used a technique that is known as moving together. The two climbers are tied together by a rope and move at the same speed. The leader runs the rope around rocky elevations or places slings on spikes and feeds the rope through carabiners attached to the slings. The rope between the leader and the seconder must always be tight. If one climber were to fall the other can hold him or her easily enough. The seconder takes out whatever gear the leader has placed. Moving together is slower than climbing without a rope but safer. It is faster than climbing in the traditional way. In a traditional climb the leader goes first, sets up an anchor at a suitable point and then brings the seconder up on a tight rope. As we moved on the narrow ridge we had drops of hundreds of metres on both sides. The views were awesome. On the left we looked down into a gigantic bowl across which were more big mountains. At the bottom of the bowl, we could see the Hesshütte we had left in the morning. At one stage we stopped at a comfortable place and ate our lunch enjoying the grand vistas.

At about 3:30 p.m. we had to descend into a small and rather airy col and then overcome a steep ascent back on to the ridge. According to the guidebook this was the most difficult move of the whole route, UIAA grade 3. The descent into the col was very exposed. Because the handholds and foot placements were poor, we abseiled into the col. I decided to lead the following steep ascent in the traditional way. I secured Willi to an anchor and he belayed me while I was climbing ahead. After I had set up a safe anchor for myself, I brought Willi up on a tight rope. This cost us some time and it was now after 4:00 p.m. There followed an easy enough ridge that led to a narrow and deep gap beyond which a steep wall rose up. I was still leading in the traditional way. Willi was about ten metres behind me and out of sight. I stepped over the gap and avoided the big wall in front by veering downward right and moving forward below the ridge for another ten metres.

When I was back on the ridge, I set up an anchor and shouted to Willi that he could follow. I could not see him but I knew that he was moving because I had to keep taking rope in. Suddenly the movements stopped. After a few minutes I heard him call: "I cannot go any further." When asking where he was, he said: "There is big wall in front of me." It dawned on me that after stepping over the gap he had gone straight ahead to the rock face instead of following the rope veering to the right. "Can you go back to the gap and follow the rope?" I shouted. "No I cannot move, I cannot turn around", came the answer. I thought of a way of climbing back to Willi and I asked him if he could build an anchor to secure himself and me. He answered in the negative. As I was leading, I had all the gear with me and he had nothing to build an anchor with. As he was unprotected and consequently could not protect me either I did not dare to climb back to him.

For some time we were weighing our options shouting to each other across the ridge. As tends to be the case in such situations time flies by at an alarming rate. My watch now showed that it was 6:00 p.m. I had a comfortable resting point and was tied to an anchor. Willi was some twenty metres behind me out of sight and unprotected. He was in his shirtsleeves and could not even move enough to get his jacket out of the rucksack. If he fell, he would fall forty metres (twice the length of the rope between us) and he might very well pull out my anchor with the force of such a fall. We had about an hour and a half of daylight left.

Should we prepare ourselves to spend the night on the rockface? For me this would not have been the first time. About twenty years earlier, Gerry Moss, an Irish friend L and myself were climbing a long route in Paklenica, Croatia. It was badly marked and we went off route and lost valuable time. By seven o'clock in the evening it was getting dark and we still had not reached the summit. We tied ourselves to the rock and spent a miserable night there. It was a warm September and we were climbing in T-shirts. The temperature did not drop below 15° C and there was no danger of us suffering from hypothermia. Occasionally Gerry burst into song. L suffered from leg cramps and he accompanied Gerry's songs with his cries of pain.

Here, in the Gesäuse it was different. The night would be very cold, and to overnight on the ridge was not an option, especially not for Willi who was in a rather precarious situation. We decided to call the mountain rescue. I had the number in my mobile phone. Luckily, I had charged it up before leaving the hut and even more luckily, I could get a signal. I dialled and an automated voice said in German "mountain rescue please wait…." After a minute or two the voice of a real (male) person came on the line and asked me for my location. When I said that we were on the Rossschweif in the Gesäuse he asked where that was! I was somewhat taken aback, but it turned out that he wanted to know which province of the country I was in. I told him that we were in Styria and he put me on to the Styrian section of the Austrian mountain rescue. Another person came on the line, asked for our precise position and told me what the procedure was going to be: It would take about 20 minutes for a helicopter of the Austrian *Alpinpolizei* (Alpine Police) to appear. We should signal to the pilot that we were the ones in need of rescue. One does this by lifting up both arms and spreading them so as to form a V. If one is not in need of rescue one lifts up one arm vertically and lets the other arm point vertically downwards. The pilot and the rescuer were to look at our situation and assess it. Then they would turn away and land outside the Hesshütte. No reason to be alarmed. After having prepared everything for our rescue they would return and first lift off the climber who was in greater danger, bring him down to the hut and then return to rescue the other one.

We now had some time at our hand. It was getting chilly and I felt hungry. I put on my fleece and ate a sandwich. The evening was glorious. The setting sun poured its light over the summits and made the rocks glow in a rosy colour. This phenomenon is known as *Alpenglühen* (alpine glow). The Hesshütte, 600 m below, was already in the shadow cast by the mountains. I could not help enjoying the situation. Poor Willi twenty metres away and out of my sight probably felt different. After half an hour the reassuring sound of the helicopter could be heard and soon it came into sight. I gave my signal indicating that we were the ones in need of help and as I had been told on the phone, the helicopter after hovering a while above the ridge turned away and landed outside the hut. Ten minutes later it took off again and approached the point where Willi was stuck. The rescuer had correctly figured that Willi was in a less safe place than myself.

Dangling on a rope about twenty metres long, the rescuer tried to get to Willi. This was a somewhat hair-raising manoeuvre. The pilot had to move close to the rocks in order to enable the rescuer to get to Willi. After a few attempts the rescuer landed beside Willi. I could not see that, but as he went out of my sight and did not come back for some time, I presumed that he was preparing to lift Willi off. The helicopter was now hovering above the ridge. Then he moved vertically up and the rescuer and Willi appeared above the ridge dangling side by side on the rope. After having delivered Willi to the safety of the hut the helicopter reappeared and the rescuer swung out to me, clipped me on a safety device and off we flew down to the Hesshütte. It was an exhilarating feeling dangling on a rope with 600 m of nothingness below me. The air blowing down on us from the blades of the helicopter felt icy cold. A few minutes later we landed outside the hut offering an entertaining spectacle to the guests.

In the safety of the hut we treated ourselves to a hearty meal and a few beers. In spite of our failure to finish the climb, our expedition was not only well worth it, but probably offered a more exciting experience than if we had reached the summit and returned to the hut without problems.

I cannot praise the *Alpinpolizei* enough. It is a remarkable organisation with highly trained pilots and mountaineers. Both, the pilot and the rescuer understood our situation very well and assured us that we had done the right thing when we called the mountain rescue. Every year about 7,600 accidents occur in the Austrian Alps. It is up to the *Alpinpolizei*, the *Bergettung* (Mountain Rescue) and other organisations of this kind to deal with them. Willi and I have the dubious honour of being included in their statistics.

13.4 From hut to hut on the Austro-Italian border 2018

Many years ago, in the early 1980s, I walked part the *Karnischer Höhenweg* with a friend. This is a 150 km long alpine trail on the border between Austria and Italy. It was an unforgettable experience. Ascending from the Sillian Hut at five o'clock in the morning for the summit of *Hochgruben* at 2,537 m above sea level to see the sunrise was awe-inspiring. Walking on from there on the ridge, in an easterly direction, in the early morning, we were above the clouds in bright sun. On our right below was the Sexten Valley on the Italian side. There was low-lying cloud in the valley so we could not see to the bottom. The Sexten Dolomites poked up above the clouds into the blue sky. It was sheer magic.

We spent four days on that route. The first day we ascended from the town of Sillian to the Sillian Hut. On day two we got as far as the Obstansersee Hut and on the third day we reached the Porze Hut. From there we descended the following day into the valley on the Austrian side and took the train back to Salzburg. The weather was glorious and I remember being brave enough to take a swim in the icy Obstanser Lake. Ever since I wanted to do this walk again and continue further east. It took me almost forty years to turn this wish into reality.

The Karnischer Höhenweg follows the World War I frontline between Austria-Hungary and Italy from 1915 to 1918. The war was also fought in the nearby Sexten Dolomites and other places. The conditions were horrendous. Both sides tried to blow each other up by undermining the mountains on which the enemy was entrenched. Terrible as the fighting was, more soldiers were killed by snow avalanches than by enemy fire. Neither side gained more than a few metres of territory. Walking the Karnischer Höhenweg and in the Sexten Dolomites the hiker frequently comes across war monuments, small war cemeteries, trenches and shelters. A particularly moving site is Monte Piano in the Sexten Dolomites. The Italian trenches and bunkers are well preserved and make for an impressive if depressing open-air museum.

One of the most spectacular places where the war was fought is the top of the *Toblinger Knoten* in the Sexten Dolomites near the famous *Drei Zinnen* (*Tre Cime*). An Austrian cannon was placed on that rather narrow top and fired at the Italian held *Paternkofel*. The summit of the Toblinger Knoten can only be reached with the help of a steep, exposed and rather exciting via ferrata. It consists of iron ropes and ladders fixed unto the rocks (*via ferrata* means iron way), enabling the mountaineer to move fairly quickly. Via ferratas were used in the war to transport men and material including heavy cannons, into places that otherwise would not have been accessible.

My Uncle Erich fought in the Dolomites in the First World War. He was in the artillery and I have a picture of him behind his cannon (see page 213). He was lucky to survive not only the First but also the Second World War. Altogether he spent about ten years of his life in active service in two world wars.

Today via ferratas have become a tourist attraction in the Alps. What was a highly dangerous affair for our forefathers over a hundred years ago has become a popular past time all over the Alps. There is a special via ferrata set with whose help the climber can attach him- or herself to the iron rope and thus move fairly safely.

In 2018 the world remembered the centenary of the end of the First World War. In Ireland, Britain and other English-speaking countries all the talk was about the Western front. Very few knew much about the Russian front and almost nobody had heard about the front between Austria-Hungary and Italy. In the summer of 2018 I set out with twelve members of my two Irish hiking clubs to walk the Karnischer Höhenweg. Today it is also known as *Friedensweg* (Peace Trail) and it is very popular among Austrians, Italians and Germans.

It was great to see the descendants of those who fought each other so viciously a hundred years ago meeting in the mountains and in the huts and getting on so well. There is a bicycle path in the Sexten Dolomites leading from Toblach in Italy to Lienz in Austria. It follows the downhill flow of the river Drau. The menus in the restaurants and cafes en-route are in German and Italian. Experiences of this kind have made me a firm believer in the European Union.

We spent six days walking from hut to hut. As the Sillian Hut was closed for refurbishment, we found shelter for the first night lower down in the *Leckfeldalm*. The next day we walked by the Sillian Hut as far as the Obstansersee Hut. Like four decades ago the weather was glorious. Although we had great views of the Sexten Dolomites we were too late to experience the sunrise on the Hochgruben that had left such a deep impression on me the first time. At the Obstansersee Hut I did not go for a swim in the lake, but two ladies of my group were brave enough to embrace the icy water. A few of us rented a rowing boat and enjoyed the views of the mountains from the middle of the lake. The next day brought us to the Porze Hut and on day three we got as far as the Hochweißstein Haus. On the fourth day we made it to the Wolayersee Hut where we stayed for two nights. The last (sixth) day was spent descending to Kötschach-Mauthen where we overnighted in a lovely hotel, with a brewery attached to it before returning, some of us to Munich and some to Vienna from where we flew back to Ireland. We could have continued walking further on the Karnischer Höhenweg, but 6 days of strenuous walking and overnighting in huts was enough for us. All the guidebooks we consulted agreed that the section we covered was the best part of the route, so we were happy with what we had achieved.

In the six days we covered a distance of almost hundred kilometres and accumulated about nine thousand metres in height. Each day required a lot of ascent over difficult alpine terrain. The most strenuous and most spectacular section of the whole route was the one between the Porze Hut and the Hochweißsteinhaus. It should only be done in good weather as it takes an average of eight hours to cover eighteen kilometres of distance and 1,200 metres of ascent. There are lots of undulations, some on very exposed and narrow paths, that can be lethal if the rocks are wet, and one certainly does not want to be caught in a thunderstorm on these high ridges. Because the weather forecast predicted thunderstorms for the late afternoon, we started at 7:00 a.m. hoping that we would finish in good time before the weather turned. We got to the Hochweißsteinhaus in good time.

Our last hut was the Wolayersee Hut. It offered the most comfortable accommodation. We got rooms for two and four persons instead of the infamous *Lager* where dozens of people sleep squashed together like sardines. As it is situated in the loveliest of locations, we stayed there for two nights. Food and drink were excellent and we had one day to explore the surroundings and return in the evening to the hut without undergoing the rigmarole of packing the rucksacks in the morning and checking into a new place at night.

Just behind the hut to the north, on an elevated spot, had been the position of the Austrian artillery during the First World War. South of the hut is a gorgeous small lake, the Wolayersee, and above its southern banks one can still see the Italian trenches and artillery positions. The Austrians and Italians fired at each other across the lake. The distance is no more than 1,000 metres. Descending from the Italian trenches in a southerly direction for five minutes one reaches the Italian hut, the *Rifugio Lambertenghi*. To walk from one hut to the other passing by the lake takes about twenty minutes.

After a good night's rest in the Wolayersee Hut we went over to the Italian side. Passing by the Rifugio Lambertenghi we descended a little further into Italy until we came to a rock face with an easy via ferrata that led to the *Cima Lastrons del Lago* in Italian or *Seewarte* in German. From there we planned to go on to another Italian hut, the Rifugio Marinelli, have lunch there and then return back to our Austrian hut. However, when we arrived at the Seewarte by 11:30 a.m. and watched the formation of threatening clouds on the horizon we decided to go back by the same way we had come. At 1:00 p.m. we stopped into the Rifugio Lambertenghi where we sat down for a lovely and leisurely lunch with plenty of wine. At about 1:30 p.m. the heavens opened and a great thunderstorm lit up the dramatic alpine scenery. We had made a good decision. By 3:00 p.m. the rain cleared and we had only a short walk back to the Wolayerseehütte for more wining and dining.

A hundred years after the ferocious fighting that took place in these mountains we could move easily, without showing a passport, from one country to the other, have lunch in Italy and dinner in Austria. I wonder what our forefathers, who were caught in the bitter conflicts of nations in the early 20th century, would have thought if they could have seen us.

On the Michelli Strobl via ferrata,
Dolomites

Wolayersee Hut, Karnischer Höhenweg

The monument marks the spot where the Austrian positions were.
The Italian positions were across the lake about 1 km away.

Austrian shelter from First World War
Sexten Dolomites

Uncle Erich in World War I in the Dolomites

A section of the Karnischer Höhenweg

Instead of an epilogue: declaration of love to Spain

Four years before the millennium Ursula had a bright idea. She anticipated that the whole world would wish to celebrate the turn from the 20th to the 21st century in an attractive location. All hotels, mountain huts and holiday homes would be booked out or unaffordable. If we acted in time, we could secure for ourselves a good place, in a prime location of our choice.

We opted for Spain. However, we had no intention of staying at the Costa del Sol, where even in winter one enjoys springtime conditions. Our choice was Segovia. This gem of a town, at the foot of the *Sierra Guadarrama* some fifty kilometres north of Madrid is famous for its well-preserved historic centre, the medieval castle and the two thousand year old Roman aqueduct. The Parador Hotel on a hill outside the town offers incredible views of the town and the surrounding mountains. Twenty friends from Ireland, Britain, Germany and Austria joined us. We all arrived before the 31st December 1999 and stayed a few days into the New Year. On 2nd January six of us ascended *La Maliciosa*, a prominent mountain in the Sierra Guadarrama. It was a cold and sunny winter day with superb views.

Spain was no random choice. It is my favourite travel destination. During my time in Glasgow, I socialised a lot with language assistants from Germany, France, Italy and Spain. I liked the Spaniards best. They were the most sociable and most fun. It was only natural that I formed a positive image of their country and that I became eager to visit it as soon as the opportunity arose. In the early seventies I travelled to Spain twice together with my first wife, Christina. We drove from Lourdes over the Pyrenees to Bilbao, Santander, Burgos, Zaragossa, Madrid, Granada, Seville and Barcelona. Franco was still in power, but his rule was coming to an end. We also undertook a short foray into Portugal where the Army had taken over and clashes between Communist and Socialist demonstrators were a daily occurrence.

As soon as we crossed into Spain I was enchanted. The earth was dry and of a reddish-brown colour, the light was harsh and of a cruel clarity. I liked the way people looked, especially the young women with their olive coloured skin, and I liked the language, which sounded as if fired from a machine gun. I fell in love with Spain before I got to know it.

Considered rationally, this is, of course, nonsense. Perhaps countries are like people. There are people whom we like instantly, others we only gradually learn to appreciate and some go down in our estimation as time goes on. We react differently to the rugged mountains of Austria, Italy or Switzerland, the endless plains of Hungary and the seascapes of Ireland or Croatia. Architecture and cultural monuments play a significant role in influencing our relationship with a country. Perhaps the most important factor is how the inhabitants of a country live and interact, in other words, the lifestyle. When I met the Spanish language assistants in Glasgow I was most impressed by the way they interacted amongst themselves and with outsiders.

Love is blind. In German we say *Liebe macht blind,* which means love *causes* blindness. Love certainly makes one overlook the negative sides of the beloved object. Spain had many negative sides when I was there for the first time. It was normal to be overcharged in restaurants. The waiters almost always made mistakes in their favour. There was a book of complaints, which the customer could ask for if he or she felt cheated. Whenever we asked for it the waiters were struck by panic and offered to reduce the bill by half. Apparently, the authorities checked these books regularly and mercilessly. In small towns and villages young men whistled behind Christina and made obscene remarks. On a beach west of Almunecar we discovered a leaking sewage pipe. When we informed the tourist office we were told not to worry as the iodine in the sea disinfected everything. In Granada we visited a young couple that Christina knew from her time as au pair girl in Spain. The woman was a staunch supporter of Franco and lived in great fear of what would happen after his death. She did not believe that the nation was ready for democracy. When we told her that we had been to Portugal she was shocked. She was convinced that Portugal would be taken over by the Communists and that Spain would follow soon.

Nothing of this diminished my love for Spain. Since then, the country has changed thoroughly. Young men no longer whistle at girls, waiters do not cheat, beaches have become clean and the population has proven to be ready for democracy. The country has become more orderly and safer without becoming boring. True, the coasts have long turned into no-go areas for the discerning traveller, as they have been completely ruined the by mindless and unregulated building that began when I was first there. However, the cities in the interior like Segovia, Salamanca, Toledo, Avila, Granada, Ubeda (to name just a few) have kept their unique charm and beauty and even improved due to careful restoration.

It is difficult to talk or write about a great love. This may well be the reason why I did not include Spain in this book. My love for Spain, however, made me interested in Latin America. I see the Spanish speaking countries of the American continent as transplantations of Spanish culture into a new environment the result of which is a fusion of the familiar European and the exotic. This applies especially to Ecuador, which plays such an important part in my memories. In contrast to the United States where the way of life of the indigenous population has been almost completely destroyed, the *indigenas* of Ecuador have kept at least some of their identity and dignity.

My travels have not yet come to an end. The older I become the more I enjoy returning to countries I have visited before and exploring them further. With increasing age I find long haul flights exhausting and therefore tend to avoid them. Yet I would love to once more visit Ecuador before I get too old. No doubt much has changed there, and hopefully for the better. It may be that I would be disappointed as I was when I visited Novi Pazar a second time. But this is a risk one has to accept. – I am still curious.